THE TUAREG

DISCARDED

ALSO BY THE SAME AUTHOR
THE APACHE INDIANS: Raiders of the Southwest
THE AZTEC: Indians of Mexico
THE CHEROKEE: Indians of the Mountains
THE CHIPPEWA INDIANS: Rice Gatherers of the Great Lakes
THE CROW INDIANS: Hunters of the Northern Plains
THE DELAWARE INDIANS: Eastern Fishermen and Farmers
THE ESKIMO: Arctic Hunters and Trappers
HORSEMEN OF THE WESTERN PLATEAUS: The Nez Percé Indians
THE INCA: Indians of the Andes
INDIANS OF THE LONGHOUSE: The Story of the Iroquois
THE MASAI: Herders of East Africa
THE MAYA: Indians of Central America
THE MISSION INDIANS OF CALIFORNIA
THE NAVAJO: Herders, Weavers, and Silversmiths
THE PUEBLO INDIANS: Farmers of the Rio Grande
THE SEA HUNTERS: Indians of the Northwest Coast
THE SEMINOLE INDIANS
THE SIOUX INDIANS: Hunters and Warriors of the Plains

THE TUAREG

NOMADS AND WARRIORS OF THE SAHARA

SONIA BLEEKER
ILLUSTRATED BY KISA N. SASAKI

WILLIAM MORROW AND COMPANY   NEW YORK 1964

Third Printing, August 1966

Grateful recognition from author and artist is given to Dr. L. Cabot Briggs of the Peabody Museum of Harvard University, for reading and criticizing the manuscript and examining the illustrations.

CONTENTS

ONE

PEOPLE OF THE VEIL

The Tuareg are a nation of nomads who live today in the central Sahara Desert in Africa. They are a dashing, freedom-loving people, who once were warriors and raiders of caravans and oases. They are also traders and the best guides across the vast wastes of the Sahara.

The Tuareg (twá-reg) never show anger or raise their voices. They are serious and thoughtful and always seem calm. With friends and clansmen they are gracious and gentle. The code of the desert calls for hospitality, even if it means sharing with friends the last skinful of always precious water. "Accept whatever life offers," the Tuareg say with dignity. So despite their reputation as fierce fighters and raiders, they are men of their word, men to be trusted.

When friends meet, they extend their hands in greeting, but they do not *shake* hands as we do. Instead, they brush the palms against each other. Then each man withdraws his hand quickly and snaps his fingers against his palm.

One man might say to the other, "Ma-tu-lid?" This means, How are you?

The reply is, "El kheir la bes," which means, Naught but good. That is, All is well.

Again the hands meet and brush each other. "Iselan?" What's new? one asks.

"La, la." No, no, is the reply. This means, No news. No news is good news.

When friends part, there are no long good-bys. People do not like to speak at parting. Again the outstretched hands flutter past each other. Then each walks away, erect and swift.

The Tuareg men are slender and tall, with spidery arms and legs. They range in height from five feet eight inches to slightly over six feet. They have thin triangular faces, broad foreheads, and pointed chins. Their waists are small, their feet and hands rather long. They are light-skinned and fine-featured, with dark eyes and straight or wavy hair. Young men cut their hair short, leaving a long lock at the crown, like an Indian scalp lock.

All Tuareg men wear veils that leave only narrow openings for the eyes. The veil in the Tuareg language is called a *tagilmus* (tá-guel-moost). Their word for people is *kel*. So the Tuareg call themselves Kel Tagilmus, People of the Veil. Their neighbors call them Tuareg. The singular for Tuareg is Targui. Some call a Tuareg woman a Targuia.

Although the veil, or *tagilmus*, may be black or white, most Tuareg veils are of a fine indigo (blue) cotton. The cloth for the veil is a long ten-foot strip about six inches wide. A man puts his veil on by first winding the cloth around his head several times, leaving a small opening at the crown. As he winds the cloth, he leaves one edge hanging over his forehead, covering his eyebrows and forming a kind of sunshade. The Targui then continues winding the strip of cloth around the lower part of his face, below the eyes. The folds over the mouth and chin are loose enough so that he can reach under the *tagilmus* without disturbing its arrangement. The Tuareg chew tobacco. This may be because it would be inconvenient to keep reaching under the veil to puff on a cigarette.

The Tuareg are not sure when or why their ancestors began to wear the *tagilmus*. Certainly, in their hot, dry homeland, the *tagilmus* is a good protection for the eyes, lips, and nostrils. Breathing against the cloth causes a circle of moist air to form around the mouth and nostrils, and prevents the skin from cracking. Some say that men could hide the ugly marks left by battle wounds under their veils and wide robes. Such marks, in addition to being unattractive, made a Targui seem less brave than he preferred to have everyone believe he was.

Up to about the age of fifteen or so, young men do not wear veils. Young men usually pluck their thin beards, but as they get older, they grow small beards and moustaches. No one ever sees their beards and moustaches, because once a man begins to wear a veil, he never takes it off, not even at home with his family.

A Targui recognizes another by his carriage and dress, perhaps by the strings of charms he wears around his neck and, quite often, by the camel he rides.

The Tuareg do not weave cloth for their robes. They used to buy all of it in the south, in the Sudan. Nowadays much of it is imported from

Europe. When new, this shiny, indigo-blue material looks almost black. In the sunlight it takes on a coppery sheen. Today indigo dye is made chemically, but it used to be obtained from plants that grow in the Sudan. This dye comes off readily. At the merest touch, it stains people's fingers, hands, bodies, faces, and feet. But the Tuareg like to have the dye rub off on their skin as it is an extra protection against the burning Saharan sun. They have, therefore, also been called Blue Men by some travelers.

The Tuareg women also wear loose, long robes, dyed with indigo. But they do not wear veils, since they seldom stay out in the sun for any length of time. They have slaves to do the housework for them and to bring in water and fuel. These servants also go out to gather wild plants, and they do the cooking. The shepherds bring in the camel and goat milk.

When a Targuia visits in the camp, she wears a large straw hat, or covers her head with a shawl or the end of her robe.

The Tuareg are a nation of close to 300,000

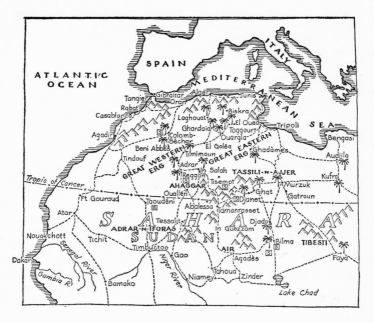

WEST AFRICA

🌴 OASIS

Ⓢ SALT MINES

---- CARAVAN ROUTES

MILES

0   200   400   600

people. Although they are divided into many tribes, there are seven main national divisions. These divisions bear geographical place names, thus identifying them with the region they call their homeland. They are: the Kel Antessar; the Kel Ahaggar; the Kel Ajjer; the Kel Air; the Aulliminden, or Iullemmeden; the Kel Adrar-n-Iforas, or Iforas; and the Udalan, Kel Gossi, and several other tribes south of the Niger River.

Each tribe is made up of many clans. The clans are further divided into groups of families. The relations between the people in these various tribal groups are regulated by an established caste system. This caste system is now deeply ingrained, and is the basis of Tuareg society. But in very ancient times the Tuareg were governed by chiefs selected by the people, because their Berber ancestors believed in governing themselves through elected officers.

The Tuareg have a class of nobles called Imochar. Next in rank come the vassals, or Imrad. Then come the Negroid serfs, who farm the oases. They are called Haratin. Lowest in rank are the household slaves, the Iklan, who live with the

Tuareg in the camps. Another class, also Negroes, are called Inaden. They are the skilled smiths, jewelers, and woodworkers.

The hard-working, settled farming serfs think a nomad's life in the open desert most desirable. They long to follow it, despite the known hardships. A recent visitor to Timbuctoo, in Mali, tells of a Haratin man, who is an excellent gardener and so has a little money to spare. He bought himself a complete Targui outfit, including a blue *tagilmus*. Nightly, after work, this man dresses up like a nomad Targui and goes out to sit in the marketplace in the center of town. The people of Timbuctoo, of course, know who he is and secretly laugh at him. But the Arab traders and the tourists stop to admire him and talk to him. The man feels he is being taken for a nomad Targui. This is his highest wish in life.

The Sahara is the biggest desert in the world, occupying a fourth of the African continent. It spreads north and south of the Tropic of Cancer and covers an area of over three million square miles. From east to west it stretches across the widest part of the continent, some 2500 miles, and measures between 800 and 1000 miles from north to south. The desert is filled with mountains, plains, canyons, and valleys—all dry except for the oases. Rainfall averages less than one inch a year. Nowhere is it over five inches a year. The soil is sand, gravel, and boulders. Sand wastes, called ergs, cover about a fifth of the entire area. These giant wastes are dangerous—blinding and burning stretches of shifting, moving sand. Wind and sand have eroded without mercy all the mountains, hills, and plains, and have carved rocks into fantastic shapes. Volcanic action piled up mountain masses, called massifs, in the southeast and the northeast. One of the largest is the Tibesti Massif in what is now Chad.

The uneven terrain adds to the hardships of traveling through the Sahara. Lack of water prevents men from using horses to any extent, since horses have to be watered daily. Camels can go without water for as many as three days, but they are poor climbers and dislike rough country. The wide, soft pads on their hooves are cut by sharp stones and are best for sandy stretches.

The rains in the Sahara are irregular. In some places it has not rained for four and six years. When rain does come, it is in a quick downpour that merely rushes over the ground and does little good. Rain has to penetrate at least a foot below the burning surface before it helps the parched land. Caravans in the Sahara avoid camping in low places for fear that just this kind of downpour may drown them or carry away precious food and clothing and other possessions.

A sandstorm does far more damage than rain. Sandstorms are much feared. Suddenly a gust of wind comes whirling across the sand. The sun is blotted out. In the haze the sand whips and lashes at men, camels, and cattle. There is no shelter from the sand in this wasteland and no place to hide and wait out the storm. One sandstorm, recorded about twenty years ago at El Goléa in central Algeria, killed 1500 goats and 2000 sheep. In the southwestern Sahara, 150 years ago, a sandstorm destroyed a caravan of 2000 men and 1800 camels. It is small consolation that the sandstorm usually dies down at sunset. It starts up again, just where it left off, on the following day.

The heat in the Sahara may rise to 130 degrees. Living things become dehydrated. If they cannot get water, they will perish. In recent times an incident occurred that might have proved fatal to a member of a French team, under the explorer of the Saharan rock paintings at Tassili, Henri Lhote. After Lhote had set up camp, a young Frenchman, named Philippe, volunteered to walk two and a half miles each way to the Tuareg city of Djanet (jah-ney). The party wanted to be in touch with Djanet for their mail and some supplies.

Philippe was told to start at dawn, which is the best time for walking, since it is still cool enough then and the sand is still firm underfoot. There is an old saying that the Sahara belongs to those who get up at daybreak. Philippe, however, started late, despite Lhote's urgings. Still he expected to cover the five miles and be back by noon. He took with him a flask of water.

Noon came and passed, and Philippe failed to return. When the clock showed two P.M., Lhote began to worry. He hoped that Philippe, trained by this time in the ways of the desert, had found a shady spot near a rock in which to wait until the sun got past midday—the hottest time of the day.

At about three P.M. a teammate came running into camp. Philippe had been found about 500 yards from their shelter. He was dying. Lhote grabbed a skinful of water and rushed to help. They applied wet towels to his head and body to cool him, while giving him sips of water. When he came to, Philippe told his story. He was on his way back from Djanet. The heat became more and more intense. Philippe was so hot and thirsty he drank all the water in his flask, although the rule of the desert is never to drain your water flask; always keep a little in reserve till you reach the next well or water hole. It was getting late and Philippe knew his teammates would worry. He, therefore, pushed on. His tongue began to swell from thirst. When he was only 500 yards from camp, he collapsed, but managed to cry out for help.

Even the toughened Tuareg have such accidents. Many perish in the desert due either to miscalculations or sheer carelessness. Men work-

ing in the desert today are allowed two gallons
of water a day per man—one gallon for cooking,
one for drinking. With great care each person in
a caravan can get along on this amount.

The secret of Tuareg endurance is that they
always move at an even pace and do not get over-
heated. Their loose, voluminous garments help
conserve body moisture, just as their veils do. The
Tuareg are thin, so they do not suffer as much as
fat people in hot weather. But no one, not even
a Targui, can survive in the desert for twenty-four
hours without water.

At sunset the temperature in the Sahara suddenly drops thirty-five to fifty degrees. A drop
from 120 degrees to 90 might be quite agreeable.
But when the temperature drops suddenly from
120 to 70, people really shiver with cold. The
Tuareg carry extra woolen blankets with them,
and wrap themselves up for the night. When
enough dried camel dung can be gathered, they
let a small fire smolder through the night to
keep their feet warm.

After rains, when the pasture turns green and
the flocks and camels have ample grass, families

of Tuareg, camping in the desert, can get along without water for a while. They drink fresh camel and goat milk. By letting it curdle and sour, they make cheeses and butter out of it. They eat dates and make a kind of cereal from millet. For nomads these are days of plenty.

There is a saying in the Sahara that after Allah had created the world and men to live in it, he had two lumps of clay left. From one, he molded a camel, from the other, a palm tree, so mankind could survive in the desert. Allah needs the desert, they say. In its peace and silence he can retreat from the noise and pressures of the world. All Tuareg feel the same way about the Sahara. It is theirs, their homeland. A woman is content to remain in her comfortable desert home the year round. A man must sometimes go to trading centers. But after visiting and trading in an oasis, a Targui is impatient to escape and return to the openness, the stillness, and the peace of the desert.

TWO

THE EARLY TUAREG

"My people," said a Targui proudly, sweeping his free left hand over the desert, "have been in this land since the beginning of the world. We came down here from the north, from far away. . . . The Arabs are a great people, too, but they have only just come into this land. . . ."

This tradition of the Tuareg tribes that they came from the north is true, although they hold no knowledge or national memories of a world other than the Sahara Desert. However, there are no written records of just when waves of Tuareg migrants did enter the Sahara. Even now this history is being pieced together from archeological diggings, from rock paintings found in the Sahara, from the related languages the Tuareg and their neighbors speak, from blood groupings, and from the memories of old people.

The ancient Sahara was a region worth fighting for. Archeologists have been digging up and studying the remains of large populations that once lived, evidently in comfort, all over it. Judging from the remains these archeologists have found, they believe the ancient Sahara was a lush region, filled with low grass valleys, trees, shrubs, and ferns. It had rivers, lakes, and swamps. Certainly it was not then called the Sahara, which means in Arabic a desert with scattered oases. What the early name of the region was we may never know.

The ancient Sahara was a fertile world, which amply rewarded its hunters, fishermen, and herders. Fishhooks and barbed harpoon points have been dug up, proving that there must have been good fishing. The harpoons no doubt were used on larger game fish. Archeologists have found pottery, pestles for grinding and crushing grain and seeds, and arrowheads. They have also found spindle whorls for spinning thread, so the people must have woven cloth.

Only one skeleton has been found in the Sahara, and it is believed to be one of the tall Negroid people, the hunters who originally lived in the region. In caves and on boulders over the Sahara, and especially in a mountainous northeastern region called the Tassili-n-Ajjer, these people and/or their descendants, left a rich heritage of rock paintings, which are considered great art today. These rock paintings show the once abundant animal life. They also reveal that the hunters must have believed in magic. A scene where a hunter is shooting an animal may have been painted by him before the hunt. He hoped that the next day he would shoot an animal while hunting, as he predicted he would in his painting. Some of the animals have square traps around their legs. So these hunters were evidently trappers, too. There are also paintings of horses, cattle, wheeled chariots, and carts.

From the archeological evidence, we are assured that the Sahara in ancient times was far from a barrier between the north and the south. In fact, it linked North Africa and the tropics. People must have crossed it continually, in all directions: north, south, east, and west, traveling and trading. As settlers from the north trekked down, the people met and mingled and prospered. There was ample room and food for everyone in the Sahara, which is much larger, for example, than the United States.

We have recently found that farming developed in the Sahara some 5000 to 7000 years ago. About 6000 years ago northern Africa began to get domesticated animals from the northeast, most likely from Egypt. The Saharans then became cattlemen, too. These early African farmers and cattlemen were mainly people of the southwestern Sudan, who lived around the headwaters of the Niger River and its big bend. They were the Mande peoples of Guinea, Voltaic peoples, and

TASSILI FRESCOES

Nigerians. They gave the world such grains as millet and the sorghums, and developed a kind of rice. They also grew peas; tuberous crops, such as Kafir potatoes; ground nuts, or peanuts; pumpkins; gourds; watermelons. The kola nut they grew furnishes us today with the ingredient that goes into cola drinks. They also raised numerous herbs, such as sesame, and grasses. Cotton, too, came originally from the western Sudan. However, it evidently spread east and reached India before it reached Egypt, which did not grow cotton until some 2500 years ago.

Some of these plants were carried by caravan and ship to East Africa, Egypt, the Middle East, and India. Later, when the slave trade developed, plants were also brought to Europe and the New World. The tamarind, grown in the southern United States, came from the Sudan, as did the oil palm. The origin of the crops was soon lost to history, but not their use. They thrived in their new homes, furnishing important foods for the world.

Then the climate of the Sahara began to change, and disaster followed. Mountains rose.

Rainfall was affected. The green, lush valleys and the rivers began to shrink and dry up. The population shrank too, and crowded into oases. By 1000 B.C. (3000 years ago) the Sahara was a desert. Thereafter, most of the invaders that came from the east and west and landed on the North African coast made no attempt to penetrate far inland.

The people who lived along the North African coastlands, the ancestors of the Tuareg, were a Caucasoid group, known as the Berbers. They had been living in North Africa for thousands of years. Six thousand years ago they were farming and using domesticated animals. Four thousand years ago they knew how to work with metals. As invaders arrived, they pushed these people into the desert.

Phoenician merchants and sailors were one group of invaders. They built cities, such as Tripoli and Carthage, and in 600 B.C. established the port of Leptis. This port became a magnificent city of marble temples, called Leptis Magna, under the Romans.

The Macedonians, under Alexander the Great,

entered only the eastern Sahara. They did, however, teach the Berbers better ways to irrigate
their crops, and the Berbers spread this knowledge
throughout the desert.

The Romans, interested in trade with the Saharan Berbers, penetrated south as far as Murzuk.
They encouraged the Berbers to breed more
camels for caravan use. Slaves, ivory, and wild
animals were brought by caravan to North African ports and traded there to the Romans. Refu-
gees from the eastern Mediterranean, fleeing
Roman oppression, began to find haven in the less
desirable interior of North Africa. With irrigation, they created oases of date palms and built
walled cities nearby.

Later the Vandals from Europe and the Turks
from the Near East forced more Berbers out of
their homelands and pushed them into the Sahara.

In the seventh century the Arab conquest of
North Africa began. The entire Mediterranean
coast, from Egypt to Morocco, felt its impact.
The Arabs called only the settled farmers on the
coast Berbers. The nomad Berbers of the Sahara
they called Tuareg.

The Tuareg say that when they moved into the Sahara they found a dark people known as Isabaten, who were living in the mountains of the Ahaggar (ah-hag'-gar). The Tuareg also say that the Isabaten were the ones who painted the Tassili frescoes. These people were poor nomadic hunters.

The Tuareg also conquered the people of the oases, deep in the Sahara. These farming people of Negroid stock were called Haratin. They were not trained for war and gave in without a struggle. In return for protection against other desert marauders, they agreed to give the Tuareg half of their garden produce. Thereafter, they continued to farm their lands as serfs. The land and water now belonged to the Tuareg conquerors.

In the days of the slave trade, from the sixteenth to the end of the nineteenth century, the Tuareg households acquired slaves. Since the Tuareg were more considerate of their slaves than were the Arabs, the slaves were loyal to their Tuareg masters and eventually began to consider themselves as Tuareg too. Slaves acted as bodyguards and companions to their masters and masters' families. They sometimes fought against Tuareg enemies as fiercely as their masters did. As repayment, the Tuareg looked after the welfare of their slaves. A man or woman slave, too old to work, was assured of a home and food by the master and his family.

As warriors and raiders, the Tuareg developed a caste system. The noble Tuareg, or Imochar, as they call themselves, were the protectors and rulers over all the Tuareg. They were the victors of fights among the Tuareg groups. The conquered Tuareg were called Imrad, or vassals, by the nobility. The Imrad paid tribute to the Imochar on the camels they raised, on their flocks of sheep and goats, and on their groves of palms and fruit trees. The Imrad fought side by side with the Imochar in wars and looked after the noblemen's camels, but they kept their own chiefs and their own councils and government.

The life of a desert nomad calls for great ingenuity. Each man pits his stamina almost every hour of the day and night against heat, sun, cold, wind, and lack of water and food. Only the strong can survive in this life. The Tuareg conquered their environment and prospered. They bred camels for mounts and for the caravan trade. They won control over caravan routes within the Sahara, and they accumulated flocks of sheep and goats for food and trade. They encouraged expansion of irrigation to grow more of their cereal—millet. Millet is the Tuareg's staple food. Dates are brought in from the oases in the north, and are a welcome luxury.

Long after the Tuareg had become desert nomads and camelmen, they, like other Berber peoples, were converted to Mohammedanism. The Tuareg, however, took on the new religion only superficially, retaining all their old customs and ways. They continued to fight and raid Arab settlements and their caravans. They also continued warring among themselves. By the twelfth century the Tuareg had carved out a large domain for themselves in the Sahara.

The Tuareg kept their own tribal governments and developed their own language, Tamahek, with their own alphabet. All Tuareg children learned to read and write some Tamahek. Since there are no pencils and paper in Tuareg homes, a

TAMAHEK LETTERING

mother writes the words in the sand, and the children learn by tracing the letters in the sand after her. Tamahek has an alphabet of some twenty-five letters, which are all consonants. There are no vowels to aid in sounding these consonants, as Tamahek has only one sign for all vowels. In addition, there are a dozen symbols that stand for two or three consonants that are always written together. Tamahek letters resemble the script of the ancient Libyans, who were neighbors of the Tuareg before they entered the Sahara. Many rocks have been found in Tuareg country that bear ancient inscriptions in Tamahek. These inscriptions are hard to decipher, because the Tuareg do not always write in a straight line from left to right, as we do, or from right to left, as Arabs do. Some inscriptions in Tamahek have been etched on the rocks in circular form, and the words run together.

The Tuareg also speak Arabic—the business language needed for the caravan trade. But sometimes, when a Targui dislikes the Arab he is trading with, he might pretend that he speaks only Tamahek, and ask his slave to translate for him.

THREE

FAMILY LIFE

In 1927 archeologists confirmed the claims of the Ahaggar Tuareg that their ancestress, their ancient Mother, Tin Hinan, was actually buried in a little tomb, guarded by long stone slabs, in the stone fortress of Abalessa. As with all legends, it is hard to separate fact from fiction, but the Kel Ahaggar say that Tin Hinan lived at Abalessa in the fifth and sixth centuries A.D. Some authors, however, believe the Tuareg entered the Sahara at a later time.

In the tomb of Tin Hinan were rich burial materials, gold jewelry, beads, bits of glass, Roman lamps, iron arm rings, and Roman coins. The coins bore the impression of Constantine the Great, who lived from about 288 to 337 A.D. Since Roman coins were found in circulation in Africa as late as the beginning of the twentieth century, the dating of the tomb cannot be based entirely on the dates of the coins found in it.

The Imochar say that this noble lady, Tin Hinan, came from the north, where they all came from, and died in the Ahaggar. The Imrad, the vassal tribes, claim that Tin Hinan's companion, a woman named Takamat, whose burial place was found a few hundred yards from Tin Hinan's, was a vassal and is *their* ancestress, *their* ancient Mother.

Descent through the mother has continued among the Tuareg since ancient times. Children, both boys and girls, belong to the clan of their mother. From their mother, they learn the names of their ancestors, and proudly recite them when they are asked who they are. But instead of saying it, as we would, "I am John Jones, an American," a young Targui will give first his father's name. "I am the son of Kelama," he might say. Then he will add, giving his mother's clan name, "And I am of the Kel Rela." This is sufficient identification for noblemen to accept him as one of them.

A Targui is taught by his mother. He learns to consider her family as his close relatives. Mother's brother is like a boy's or girl's second father.

As might be expected, children of sisters— that is, cousins—are very fond of each other. Mother's brother's children are cross-cousins, since they belong to a different clan—the clan of the uncle's wife. With cross-cousins, one is permitted to have fun. Cross-cousins are as fond of each other as the other cousins, but the relationship is different. A boy can play all sorts of tricks on his cross-cousin and never be reprimanded. A cross-cousin must never be offended with another cross-cousin, no matter what he does. A boy cross-cousin may tease his girl cross-cousin, pull her hair, or spoil the leather-and-straw mat the girl has been plaiting. She will not get angry or complain to her mother. But, when she gets a chance, she will play a few tricks on her boy cross-cousin and expect him to show the same good grace, good manners, and patience. Cross-cousins fight, as all children do, but must never show malice or anger. In this way they learn to get along with one another and to appreciate one another. Often a young man decides to marry his cross-cousin, the girl with whom he played as a youngster. A Targui can also marry his cousin—that is, his mother's sister's daughter—even though both of them belong to the same clan.

A boy's father's relatives are his cousins, too. The children of brothers often live in the same camp and play together. The children of brothers are also permitted to marry.

A nobleman usually marries a girl of a noble clan. Their children belong to her clan, and so they will be noblemen too. However, should a noble Targui marry a Targuia from a vassal clan, an Imrad, his children will be counted as Imrad like their mother, not noblemen like their father. On the other hand, if a noblewoman marries an

Imrad, their children will be considered noble like her. Not many noblewomen marry Imrad men, though, for there are enough noblemen to choose from. Girls of noble clans are raised to expect noblemen for husbands.

This practice of claiming descent through the mother is called matrilineal descent. Among the Tuareg women are very important. Other Moslems—that is, the believers in the teachings of Mohammed—do not respect women as the Tuareg Moslems do. This is one of the main reasons for the belief among scholars that the Tuareg, in their ancient days, had another religion. They may have been Christians. The design of the cross is widespread among them. Among the Moslems, for example, a man may marry more than one woman; many Moslems are polygamous. The Tuareg are monogamous; they have only one wife.

Since Tuareg women are very much respected, they enjoy equality in the household with the men. The head of a household consults with his wife on all important decisions. He trades the camels and livestock only after talking to her. This behavior is more like that of Christian families than Moslem.

Among most Moslems, girls have no say in the selection of the men they will marry. Among the Tuareg, young men and women meet at special parties and festivals. They see each other openly and make their own decisions about their future mates. There are two main festivals for young unmarried people. These courtship gatherings are called Tendis and Ahals.

A Tendi party is held during the day. It usually follows another festive occasion, such as the naming of a child, a boy's initiation ceremony, or the feast that follows the collection of tribute due a nobleman from his farmer serfs. The Tendi gets its name from a tall wooden drum. The base of the drum is a mortar, used for crushing seeds and grain, with a piece of leather stretched over its mouth. Young women gather around it in a circle. They are all dressed in their best, their faces painted, their eyes accentuated with heavy black eye shadow, and their hands and toenails hennaed. Two ladies sit on the poles, connected to the drum, and make it sound. One woman sings and recites

verses, while the others clap in rhythm. The singing is in a high falsetto. It is more like a whine
or a wail, and in the openness of the desert it has
a strange haunting quality.

The singing goes on and on for hours. Some
of the songs are old; some are improvised. Tuareg
girls are trained by their mothers to recite poetry
and sing. They can make up poems and songs on
the spur of the moment.

After a while young men, dressed up in their
best, begin to arrive on their camels. The singing
does not stop with their coming. The young men
dismount and form groups behind the women
singers. The young people all know one another,
and the men sit down next to the girls of their
choice. Married women may join the singing, if
they are needed, but everyone knows they are
married, and the young men are not interested in
them. When an especially familiar song is sung,
requiring no special attention, the young people
whisper among themselves, so there is a running
murmur of talk with the singing.

The sun begins to set, and it starts to cool off.
The singing stops. Now it is the men's turn to

show off. They jump up and mount their camels, forming two lines. As a rule, the Tuareg ride their camels at a walk. But on this festive occasion the men make the camels prance back and forth between the two lines to show off their riding before the ladies. They next form one line and whirl around and around, faster and faster, ever closer to the circle of women huddled around the drum.

One young man comes racing, bends down, snatches a shawl from a girl's head, and dashes off with it. The others race after him trying to recover the shawl. They finally catch up with him and slowly return to the circle of laughing women. The shawl is returned to its happy owner. The girl is pleased that she has been thus selected, and knows that the young man likes her.

It is getting dark by now and growing cold. The men dismount to say good-by to the women and to thank them for the singing. They then disperse to their various camps on the vast desert.

Poetry, music, and dance go together, and perhaps years ago Tuareg men and women danced, too. Today, however, the women never dance, although a man will sometimes get up at a gathering and do a sword dance while a friend beats a drum. With arms overhead, the dancer holds up his sword and begins by running toward the drum. Then he circles around the drum in rhythm to its beat.

All sorts of entertainers—singers, musicians, men with puppet shows, clowns, magicians with special tricks—visit the Tuareg camps. The chief of a camp plays host to the entertainers. As soon as word of their arrival gets around to the neighboring camps, people come to see and hear them.

An Ahal party is held at night. The usual occasion for such a gathering is the arrival of a famous female singer. Such female singers are generally handsome, middle-aged women, who are well-known throughout Tuareg camps. The lady musician sits down at sunset in front of her tent. She accompanies herself on a single-stringed musical instrument, made of a half gourd covered with leather. Her voice, like those of the other Tuareg women, is high-pitched and haunting. The audience enjoys especially her romantic songs concerning a hero warrior or a famous camel. While she sings, she sizes up her audience and then begins to improvise. She may make up a song on the spot about a pretty young Targuia she sees in the audience. This delights everybody, including the young lady.

When the singer pauses, people move about greeting one another and talking. The host has bowls of milk passed around as a refreshment. Each man lifts his veil with one hand, takes a sip from the bowl, and hands it to the next person.

Afterward the Ahal breaks up into small groups. The women usually do the talking, and the men enjoy listening to them. In most cases, the women are better educated than the men. They all know how to read and write Tamahek, and can recite poetry and make up poems of their own. As boys, the men also learned to read and write Tamahek, but they do not practice it as much as the women do, and so tend to forget how to read and write their own language.

At the end of the party, couples wander off to be by themselves. Kissing is permitted, but many couples prefer to rub noses instead.

Tuareg men marry late. A young Targui has to own quite a few camels to help pay the bride price, and he must accumulate a large enough flock to feed his family and have extras to sell to buy household needs.

When a young couple decides to get married, the man sends over to her parents some small gifts and declares his intentions toward their daughter. If he is accepted, the man's parents help him with the bride price of several camels, which he has to present to the girl's parents. The expression bride wealth is more appropriate than bride price, since a Targuia's parents usually give their daughter many more camels as their marriage gift to her. These are mixed with her husband's herds, but they remain the wife's personal property, and she keeps track of them. In case of a divorce, or if her husband dies, a Targuia can take her property with her when she leaves her husband's camp. Since the children belong to the mother's clan, they also go with her, and they will inherit the livestock.

As a rule, a young couple lives with the bride's family for about a year. However, a young Targui is more at home with his own relatives. He has grown up with them and knows everyone well. His relatives will gladly help him when he is in need. After the year is up, if the husband wishes, they join the camp of his people. But if husband and wife belong to the same clan, they remain with their people no matter which household they live in. The decision as to where to live is up to the man, who is head of his household.

The marriage customs among noblemen and vassals are the same. However, when a slave wishes to marry, he or she must get the master's permission. This permission is usually granted, especially if the couple works for families that camp near each other. In most cases the master will give the slave the necessary bride price for his bride's parents.

The children of slaves and masters grow up together and play together, but as they get older the children of slaves begin to work as herders. The boys learn to care for the master's sheep, goats, and camels. The girls are taught to work in the household.

A Tuareg camp is serene and peaceful, its activities unhurried. Life flows slowly and evenly. During the day the Sahara is blinding. The blazing sun drains everything of color. People continually shade their eyes. They walk or ride in the daytime only when they have to. Women keep busy inside their tents. With sunset the desert awakens to breathtaking beauty. The surroundings—the sky and mountains—turn red, afire with color. As the light fades, the earth takes on a golden glow, and turns blue and purple with the sun's last rays. Night falls. Suddenly a thousand stars brighten the indigo sky. They hang from the sky like large gold beads. Tuareg families move their mats in front of their tents. They sit and watch this wonderful sight nightly. At such times they must love their desert home.

Men usually leave home at dawn to tend their flocks and to see that everything is in order. Every few days the men must go out to look for new pasture, especially during the dry season. Some men, who work as guides for caravans, may be away from home for weeks or months at a time. Some are away on trading trips.

The little red-leather canopies of the Tuareg

tents proclaim to those in the Sahara that these
are Tuareg homes and none other. A tent is usually set up away from the pasture, since slaves
carry the water for the household, and the lady
of the house need not worry about conserving her
own energy. She stays inside the tent with her
small children during the hot part of the day.
The place chosen for a tent is on high ground in
case of rain, but a man directs his tent to be set
up in an inconspicuous place. It is usually surrounded by boulders.

The ground is leveled off for the floor, and the
tent is firmly pegged down on three sides, with
the front left open. The front usually faces the
east, the rising sun. Its warming rays, after the
chilly Saharan nights, are most welcome. The
tent cover used to be made of tanned mouflon
(wild sheep) skins, which the women of the
household sewed together skillfully with strips of
colored leather and fringe. Nowadays mouflon
skins are rare, and tent covers are made of thirty
or more tanned goatskins or, less often, sheep-
skins, dyed a coppery red. The huge tents of the
wealthy Tuareg use up to a hundred skins.

The inside of a Tuareg tent is very simple. The roof is supported on a wooden frame and slopes toward the back. The average size of a tent is about ten feet deep and ten to fifteen feet wide. Because the roof at the back of the tent is low, the space there is reserved for family possessions. The women's belongings and household goods are on the left side. They are packed into leather bags of all sizes, which the women skillfully make and decorate with fringes and designs of many colors. The men's possessions—extra clothing, blankets, ammunition—are on the right side. These, too, are kept in colorful leather bags and pouches decorated with fringes and designs. When a man comes home, he puts his saddle inside the tent on the right. These possessions further reduce the small space for family living.

The average household can pack its goods on the backs of two camels, while a donkey or two carry the odds and ends. Donkeys are more sure-footed than camels, and a woman may prefer to pack her precious clay cooking pots on the back of one of them. But a donkey can carry only about 100 pounds while a camel can carry from 250

to 600 pounds. Nomads, who have to move their homes every few weeks, try not to get too burdened with possessions. When it is time to leave, the less property a family has, the easier it is to load up the camels and donkeys and get settled in the next camp for another few weeks.

A wall of matting, which is made up of thin reeds and plaited mats about three to four feet high, circles the inside of the tent. These mats, also made by the women, are usually attractively decorated with colored geometric designs and strips of leather. Although they are over twenty feet long, they can be rolled into neat packs for

moving. The two ends of the matting extend outside the entrance of the tent, forming a patio. In the early evening the family sits there drinking cups of hot, sweet tea.

The rest of the inside furnishings of a tent are very simple, too. The people sleep anywhere inside the tent on floor mats. The floor of the tent is always clean. A servant sweeps up the sand several times a day and spreads out fresh sand. Most people sit on mats on the floor, although the wealthier people have rugs.

A large waterskin hangs just outside the patio entrance. Cooking is done by a servant in the open nearby. The cooking utensils consist of a few pots and bowls. There is usually a wooden mortar and pestle for crushing seeds and grain. Many families also use a stone quern for crushing grain. The quern is made up of two round millstones. A peg from the bottom stone fits through a hole in the center of the top stone, and thus holds them together. Grain is poured through the center hole of the top stone onto the stone beneath. As the upper stone turns, with the aid of a handle that is attached to it, it crushes the grain, which is gathered from the edges of the lower millstone.

Most Saharan people eat with their fingers, but the Tuareg use wooden spoons, dipping them into a pot or a wooden bowl. While eating, a man holds his veil away from his chin with his left hand and spoons food into his mouth with his right.

In a Tuareg camp the camels and goats furnish most of the food. When camel milk is fresh, it has a very sweet flavor. People drink both fresh and sour camel and goat milk, and they eat dried cheese made from this milk. Goat milk is churned in skins to make butter. The people use the butter to flavor their hot cereals, made with millet flour. The Tuareg also bake little flat cakes, made of millet and ground wild seeds.

Couscous is a famous Tuareg dish. It is a sort of stew, with tiny grains of dough rolled from barley or millet, cooked with vegetables and butter. Sometimes meat is put into the couscous. But nomads, as a rule, do not care to slaughter animals just for food, so meat is seldom eaten.

The tent is home most of the time. Only in very hot weather, when a family plans to stay in one place for a while, do they move to a *zeriba*. The *zeribas* are cubical huts of poles and grass through which the air can circulate. These huts are cooler and offer better shade from the sun. Smaller and poorer tents, lean-tos, and *zeribas* behind the master's tent are the homes of the slaves and herders.

Tuareg women are slender, and shorter than the men. At home they usually wear a wide one-piece garment of indigo-blue cotton that covers them to the ankles. Their ornaments are bead necklaces and silver earrings and bracelets. A big shawl, also indigo, is kept in the back of the tent

to be used when they go out. The women devote
a great deal of time to caring for their hair—
greasing, combing, and plaiting it. They put yel-
low, red, or white clay on their cheeks and foreheads, which they claim keeps them cool, and
paint dark shadows around their eyes.

The life of a noble Targuia is not as comfortable as it would be inside a permanent, well-
furnished home, but the women are happy with
their lot. They have a great deal of time for
themselves and for their children. Since the
housework is done for them, the women keep
busy plaiting mats, making leather pouches, cords,
whips, and bridles for their husband's camels.
These are works of art and show much patience
for detail. The women do not weave at all, and
the tailors are either Arabs or Negroes. But, then,
neither the women's clothing nor the men's re-
quires much tailoring.

A man's costume begins with a pair of wide
trousers, which are held around the waist with a
leather cord. The seat of the trousers is very baggy
and hangs down below his knees. The legs are
narrow at the bottom and fit tightly around the

ankles. A man wears a long white cotton shirt with very wide sleeves that reach just below his elbow. One flowing garment, made of white cotton, is just a wide piece of cloth, seven to eight feet wide and eight to ten feet long. In the middle of it is a V-shaped opening for the head. This garment is a *gondoura* (gan-doó-ra). The bottom and sides are left open, and only the corners are sewed together. The *gondoura* covers a man's arms. To free them, he rolls it up on his shoulders. A large pocket, the only one a man has on his person, is sewed on the inside of the *gondoura*. Over this white *gondoura* a man wears another one, similarly styled, made of shiny indigo-blue or black cotton. On festive occasions Tuareg men used to wear over the two *gondouras* a third one made of very narrow loomed strips of material, dyed in bright stripes of white, violet, pink, and dark blue.

The Tuareg men sometimes wind a strip of cloth around their waists and stomachs, and hold it in place by slipping a width of the cloth over the shoulders. It is wound over the shirt and trousers before a man puts on the white *gondoura*.

Each man carries on the side of his saddle a woolen blanket or a woolen garment, which he puts on at night. The wide Arab cloaks with hoods, called burnouses, made of camel's hair or wool, are so comfortable and warm that more and more Tuareg wear them when they can afford to buy them.

The Tuareg men wear jewelry only for special events, but they usually wear a silver ring on one finger and an arm ring or two. The arm rings are made of stone. At first the stone is greenish, but after it is boiled in fat it turns black and shiny. A man wears an arm ring above the right elbow, and sometimes he wears a ring on each arm. The origin of these rings is not certain. Some say they have magical properties. They say that scrapings from such a ring, when sniffed up the nose like snuff, will stop a nosebleed. Young bloods have their rings inscribed by their fiancées. It may be that this custom is a carry-over from the time of Tin Hinan.

Nomad mothers, as a rule, have no trouble giving birth to babies. When it is time for a woman to give birth, the tent is partitioned, and she rests quietly in her compartment. She remains there with the infant until she fully recovers. The baby stays inside the tent, cared for by a servant, while the mother goes out on short visits. On longer visits, the mother carries the baby with her inside her cloak, since she has to nurse it. Women nurse their babies for at least eighteen months, more than twice as long as most mothers in the United States or in Europe.

Tuareg babies are usually healthy and happy. They seem to have little difficulty in making the change from mother's milk to adult foods. Elsewhere in Africa, where the adult diet is poorly balanced and lacking in proteins and fats, babies develop all sorts of stomach troubles and skin infections. In such places it is not unusual for a mother to lose two out of every three children she bears. The Tuareg parents are more fortunate in this respect.

Because the Tuareg children stay indoors so much, they wear no clothing at all for the first few years. In its early life, a baby is bathed frequently. Older children and adults bathe only

when they get to a river or a water hole, since
water is very scarce. A Targui enjoys a good
splashing and scrubbing in the water as much as
anyone else, but the chances for frequent bathing
do not exist in the Sahara. Besides, repeated bathing dries the skin and makes it crack in the hot
desert air.

People have remarked how beautiful Tuareg
children are. The little girls have long hair and
lovely eyes and skin. Their dark eyes are striking,
because their mothers rub dark eye shadow around
them. Little boys have most of their hair cut
short, leaving a scalp lock on the crown or a lock
on either side of the head over the ears.

Children are watched all the time as they play
inside the tent or at its entrance. There are poisonous insects on the Sahara that may kill a child.
A scorpion's bite may not be fatal to an adult, but
it is fatal to a child. Scorpions and other insects
hide under mats. That is another reason mats are
shaken out and the tent floor swept so often.

When a child gets older, the mother begins to
teach it to read and write Tamahek. The mother
either recites from memory or reads long poems

to her children. The children often memorize them and are encouraged to compose poems of their own. In the evening, when the family gathers together, the children recite the poems they have learned. The father is very pleased to listen and thoroughly enjoys the recitations. A little girl learns to play the simple one-stringed instrument of the Tuareg and to accompany herself on it as she sings. This, too, is enjoyed by parents and visitors. The mother also teaches her children all she knows of Tuareg folklore and especially her own clan's history.

In the old days this completed the schooling of Tuareg children. On the very rare occasions when a Moslem holy man came to visit a camp, he read to the boys from the Koran, which was all the religious instruction the boys received. Girls were not considered worthy of such instruction.

More recently Tuareg children were urged to attend school and to learn a European language, usually French. The French government sent teachers to follow nomad camps. A teacher set up school in a tent. All the children, whether noble or not, were welcomed into these one-room school tents.

Tuareg fathers have no objections to their children going to school, but they themselves are not much interested in learning French. Yet the Tuareg are not ignorant of the world. Because the men travel south into the Sudan with caravans and trade in the oases, they are well informed. They know something about Europe. They are good listeners, remember well the things they hear, and talk of them with enthusiasm and intelligence.

Under the guidance of both parents, children learn proper behavior and manners. When given something, a Targui boy will first offer it to his father, then to the other adults in the tent, before he feels free to keep it for himself. One Targui boy was given a knife as a present. His eyes lit up with pleasure. But he did not even open it to test the blade, which any youngster would do almost automatically. Instead he merely moved his open palm, into which the knife had just been placed, toward his father, and offered the gift to him with the poise and dignity of an adult.

Even though the Tuareg are nomads, a child does not see very much of the outside world at an early age. Most families live and move within a certain territory, where they camp at different times of the year. There is always the danger of heat or of sandstorms, so youngsters are not encouraged to wander off by themselves. Their whereabouts are always known. That is why every boy looks forward to being taken on a journey by caravan. At last he will see the Saharan world for himself.

But before that, when a boy is between five and seven, he is circumcised, and undergoes the first initiation into manhood. The time for the circumcision is set when there are several boys of the right age—whether of noblemen, vassals, or slaves —in the camp or in adjoining camps. In one of the camps there is usually a man who is experienced in performing circumcisions and who operates on all the boys of all ranks at the same time. The wounds are covered with fat and bandaged. After a few days the boys go out together and sit in the hot sand, which is soothing and which is believed to help the healing. This experience together cements friendships that last a lifetime. The boys feel that they all belong to a special group—an age set.

At the initiation ceremony that follows cir-cumcision, a boy receives gifts. A fond uncle, mother's brother, may even give the boy a camel, but usually he will give him a hairy sheep or a few goats. The animals will herd with the boy's father's flocks, but are considered the boy's property. This is the beginning of a boy's acquiring some wealth of his own. Later his father or another kinsman will present him with a sword. The boy will spend much time practicing with it. A Targui does not consider himself a man unless he owns a knife and sword.

The games boys play are limited by the heat, sand, and gravel of the Sahara and by the scarcity of toys and materials. For example, the boys play a game that resembles our field hockey, but the ball and hockey sticks are entirely homemade. Each boy uses a stick made from a sapling, which has been peeled and shaved so that the lower end is thicker and slightly bent. The ball is the size of a tennis ball and is made of pieces of cotton stuffed and sewed into a piece of heavy cloth. Dr. L. Cabot Briggs, who saw the boys of the Ahaggar play the game, reports that they divide into two groups. The game is played without marked goals or scorekeeping. Each boy, when he gets the ball, tosses it up and tries to get several whacks at it before another player can get possession of it. They play until they are tired or have to seek cover from the heat.

After the age of ten a boy begins to go out with his father and with the herders to acquire the skills of adult life. The son of a nobleman works side by side with the herders. He learns to ride a camel. He learns to care for the camels and flocks and learns what to do to cure some animal diseases.

Later the young Targui is taken by his father on a long journey with a caravan. Whether they are noblemen or vassals, boys in caravans run errands for older men, gather camel dung for fires, and fetch water. A boy learns to make a fire by rubbing a small green stick, about six inches long and sharpened at one end, against a dry stick. He keeps rubbing in a straight line, pushing the sharpened stick back and forth, until he forms a groove. The dry dust and fiber collect at one end of the groove, and the friction ignites them. Having learned to make a fire in this primitive way, so that he will not be helpless in an emergency, the boy may begin to use matches or, more likely, flint and steel.

At night, while the men sleep, the boys take turns standing watch. This is good training and toughens them for manhood and for a lifetime in the Sahara. Although a Targui nobleman does not care to do manual labor, he is wise enough to know that for his son to survive he must be able to cope with anything a man alone in the desert might have to face. By the time a boy is fifteen he is ready to go out into the desert and do a man's work. After a few years, at another ceremony, he will receive a veil, a *tagilmus*, and will wear it for the rest of his life.

FOUR

CARAVANS AND RAIDS

A Targui on his camel is like a king on his throne. The saddle is narrow and light, and is covered with red and black leather that has been carefully tooled in geometric designs. Its V-shaped frame of wood fits over the camel's withers. The rider sits on a rounded seat with a backrest. The front of the saddle, the pommel, is built up high and is designed in the shape of a cross, like the hilt of a Tuareg sword. These saddles are so valuable to the Tuareg that they never part with them. When camping, each man keeps his saddle beside him while he sleeps.

A Targui is at his best when he is mounted on a camel. He guides it with a single narrow leather rein that is attached to a hole in the camel's right nostril and passed under its jaw to the left. The rein is often a gift from his mother, his wife, or his sister. The Tuareg women plait these reins of ten or a dozen strips of tanned and dyed leather that are as fine as thread. It takes skill to cut such fine leather strips with a knife. They do not use scissors. The plaited rein, like the saddle, lasts a long time.

Riding camels carry only one passenger and light equipment for the rider. These tall, fine-boned animals are so specialized they are never required to carry heavy burdens. A rider's equipment is an extra cloak or a blanket, a small skinful of pressed dates, a skinful of water, and a copper bowl. To make a waterskin, a goatskin is carefully peeled off its carcass and the holes sewed together. It is well oiled and greased or tarred, and so the water from a fresh goatskin tastes of tar and of goat or sheep's fat. But as the goatskin is used, the water gradually loses this unpleasant taste. When traveling, the water evaporates a bit from the skin, which keeps it cool and refreshing to a thirsty man in the hot desert.

The knife each man carries is part of his dress, and stays on his person at all times. A man wears it on a leather cord, slung across his chest.

The double-edged Tuareg sword is three to three and a half feet long, and the hilt is shaped like a cross, but it is seldom carried nowadays. Good swords are prized and kept in handsome leather sheaths. Since the Tuareg themselves do not work with metals, they either inherit the swords or trade for them with outsiders. Usually each sword has a long history behind it, which its owner is happy to relate around the evening campfire.

A Targui's knife, however, is an indispensable tool for traveling. It is always with him. He may also carry a dagger, which some men fasten to the inside of the forearm with a leather band. To use his dagger, a man merely grasps its cross-shaped handle with his other hand to release the blade.

Nowadays a man also carries a rifle and some rounds of ammunition.

In the old days a warrior carried a huge shield, two and a half feet by four and a half feet. The shields were of hide, usually of Oryx-antelope skins, because they are tough. These hides were tanned and dried in the sun for extra toughness. When not in use, the shield was hung from the saddle. Shields are not in use today, as they offer no protection against firearms.

Men used to practice with their swords as we practice fencing. Two men, protected by their shields, parried back and forth, lunging and retreating. Some used to practice while mounted on their camels, which takes even greater skill, since camels are notoriously hard to manage. However, the patient warriors trained cow camels for this. Cow camels are more submissive than the males.

The Tuareg are excellent camel breeders, because they are most patient and considerate of their mounts. The camel has been called the ship of the desert. Even today, in our age of helicopters, jets, and supertrucks, camelback is still the safest and cheapest way to travel in the Sahara.

Camels have been in the Sahara for at least twenty centuries. The Saharan camel is a single-humped, long-necked, long-legged animal with a small head, small ears, tough lips, sharp teeth, and a strong stomach. It originally came from the Middle East, where it is called a dromedary. *Dromedary*, a Greek word, means *to run*. This is obviously a misnomer, for the camel prefers an even walking pace. The African camel is related to the Bactrian camel of Central Asia, which has two humps. When an African camel travels on short rations, its hump, which is stored fat, shrinks as some of the fat is absorbed. In color, it ranges from near black through buff, brown, and gray to eggshell white. Some are white with huge gray spots, and have one brown eye and one blue. The Tuareg choose young near-white camels for training as mounts.

The camel is well equipped for desert travel. Its nostrils are lined with hair and can be completely closed. The heavy lashes protect the eyes against desert sand. The camel's feet are cloven, with broad, thick, flat pads underneath, to make walking on sand easier. It also has a horny pad on its chest, which is essential for sleeping on hard ground.

Although cow camels are not as strong as the males, they are nonetheless welcomed in caravans. They are more docile, and offer their owners the extra luxury of fresh milk en route. Should a cow camel calve during a trip, the small calf is placed on its back for two or three days, until it is strong enough to keep up with the rest. With its calf beside it, the camel readily lets a man milk it.

Camels need care and constant attention. If overworked or injured, they begin to lose their vitality. The camelman's watchful eye sees these warning signals. He can correct them in time by taking the load off a camel and caring for its wounds. Otherwise, the camel will suddenly, without warning, drop dead. Not only is this loss costly, but the dead camel's load has to be distributed among the other pack camels, which are already fully loaded.

While in a caravan, camels may be watered every third day. When nearing a well, the guides work the schedule out so that they reach the stop at midday, when it is hottest. The caravan then takes a long rest, and the camels can drink their fill. A camel is at its thirstiest and so will drink the most at this time of day. Within ten minutes it can make up for all its water loss. Were a person to drink that much at one time after a long thirst, it would be suicide. But a camel is so constructed that it can fill up safely and then go without water for another three days. A camel can lose thirty percent of its body water without harm. A man will die if he loses only twelve percent.

A camel is more comfortable walking in the hot sun than a man is. Its coarse hair insulates its body, but permits air to circulate against its skin, so sweat evaporates easily. A camel's temperature rises slowly during the heat of the day. At night its temperature gradually goes down. So a camel is also more comfortable during the cold Saharan nights than men are.

When there is ample green grass, camels need not drink any water at all. The moisture in the grass is enough to satisfy them. Green grass is favored as fodder, but a camel will eat almost anything a goat will eat—twigs, shrubs, and even the four-inch-long thorns of the flat-topped African trees, called acacias.

Camelmen load each camel only once a day. The strain on a camel to rise on its long, thin, stiff legs while carrying a heavy load is very great, so the animal is not required to do it more than once a day, except in an emergency.

All packsaddles must be light, so the camel can carry the maximum load. The saddle is a simple contraption, an inverted V-shaped piece of wood, lined underneath, with a flat board on each side of the V. The saddle fits over the camel's shoulders and hump. Two mats, or two sacks stuffed with grain, cushion it against the animal's body. A goatskin, stuffed with the camelman's supplies, is tied to the back of the saddle and forms a rear pad. The camel's sloping hind quarters are weak, so loads must be carried forward, where the weight can be absorbed by the shoulders and hump.

No camel is so well domesticated that it does not protest at being loaded. Loading is a daily struggle that sorely tries the camelmen's patience and endurance. At dawn, long before the day's journey is to begin, the men, working in pairs, remove their cloaks and start loading the camels.

To make sure that the camel does not suddenly stand up before its load is tied securely and crash it to the ground, a man ties a loop around the camel's knee, which keeps its leg bent. The men throw the empty packsaddles on its back and then, straining, each takes his share of the bulky load of 200 to 300 pounds, staggers, and lifts it to the sides of the saddle. The men carefully balance the loads on each side and fasten them with ropes to the short wooden pegs on the packsaddle.

The loading completed, a man pulls the knot

from the camel's knee. The camel unfolds itself and staggers up. However, this movement is often so jerky that the load may become unbalanced and slip to the ground, saddle and all. The loading is then repeated. Again the camel's knee has to be tied. Again the men stagger, each with his half of the load, hoping nothing was damaged by the drop. Finally the camel rises safely and remains standing with its load. The two men then proceed to load the next camel. In a caravan of several hundred camels, loading is a time-consuming, exhausting chore for everyone. And it has to be done daily.

In the meantime, the loaded camels begin to graze in the last bit of pasture before the start. As they crane their long necks down, close together, they naturally bump into one another. The wide loads swing and squeeze together, some become unbalanced, and others are dropped entirely. Once more the camelmen have to reload. For every hundred camels thus loaded, about ten have to be reloaded each day. However, this method of loading a camel makes unloading at night simple. As the camel kneels, a man pulls out the knots in the tie rope, and the load drops on either side of the animal. Freed of its load, the camel gets up and wanders off to pasture.

The sight of loaded camels and riders, passing across the empty horizon, is a beautiful, heart-warming sight indeed in the lonely, lifeless desert wastes. The men, as they walk their camels, guide them over ground that is free of stone. From time to time a man bends down and tosses a rock from the trail onto the mounds of stones other camel-men before him have built up. This is a helpful custom, since it not only clears the caravan route, but serves as a marker for those who follow. A specially shaped mound of stones may commemorate a holy man, who stopped there long ago and, according to Moslem custom, prostrated himself in prayer. Such a mound is held sacred and is left undisturbed, even by those who are not of the Moslem faith. Stones, spaced in a special way, warn the caravan leader of an approach to a narrow passage between hills, and guide him to it. The camels and their drivers need to be especially cautious in such places.

A caravan is like a city on the move. It is more

self-sufficient than the pioneer wagon trains that once crossed the continent of North America, but the journey is filled with hardships. A caravan today cannot rely on hunting for extra food, as our pioneers did in the past. It must find water en route, and the men must plan for their return journey. Those who undertake such trips across the Sahara have to make sure they will survive. They also have to make a profit for themselves, for the many different men who own the camels, and for the merchants of the cities behind them and ahead of them, who own the trade goods they carry. The men, the camels, the goods, and the guides come from a hundred different points in and out of the Sahara, and will eventually have to return to these points—in a month, in two, or in five. They will settle accounts, rest up, and then begin to plan another caravan journey.

Caravans have been crossing the Sahara for at least 5000 years, but experience has not made crossing it easier. The route at best is rubble-strewn. Even on level ground, the camelmen have to keep an eye on each camel, to see that the load stays put and rides well. A sharp stone may cut a camel's footpad, which begins to bleed. The driver has to spot this before the crack widens and the camel begins to limp. Men have to inspect the pasture before turning the camels out to graze. A camel may eat some poisonous plant and die. Its skin may develop sores due to insect bites or be irritated by the packsaddle.

Many of the camel owners today are impoverished Tuareg, whose total wealth is one or two camels. Some men own only part of a camel. Each hopes the camel will return safely from a trip and that he will be able to pay off his friends with the profit he will get, and so own the whole camel. Again, if all goes well, this camel will bring in more profit several months later after another expedition. Its owner may then buy part of another camel. His life's savings are thus concentrated in one camel. Should the animal die on the trip, he might be paid back what it is worth, but no more. If the caravan should perish, he will have lost everything. Therefore, the owner is happy when a friend hires himself out with a caravan and promises to keep an eye on his camel.

Tuareg serve as caravan guides, since they

know the routes well. A Targui nobleman who
acts as a guide is not *hired* as a vassal might be.
He is *invited* to help out as a guide, is furnished
with a riding camel, if he needs one, and is
offered a share of the expected profits. A Tuareg
guide knows every landmark on his route and
assumes full charge of a caravan. His orders are
to be obeyed. If there have been recent raids on
the route, the guide may bring along some of his
own kinsmen and armed vassals. Although more
people will have to share in the profits, the caravan will thus be safe. Guides are resourceful men,
and have saved many lives and goods under their
protection.

There have been instances when the merchants
who owned the caravan goods disagreed with the
guide over the route he preferred or the time of
travel he chose. The guide does not carry a map
of the region. He has the route firmly fixed in
his memory. If the owners insist on night traveling, the guide may go along with their wishes.
At night he can guide the caravan by the stars,
with which he is usually familiar, and it is far
more comfortable to travel in the cool of night,

and easier, because the sand is firm. At other times, however, the guide may prefer to travel in the daytime, so he can see his landmarks and keep a lookout for possible raiders.

A caravan faces many crises daily. When a steep path leads up onto a plateau or when a pass lies through a gorge, the camelmen are alerted to trouble ahead and stand ready to help the camels. The men push and prod and encourage them to make the grade.

In the central Sahara it rains very seldom, but rains may fall in summer or in winter. If a downpour catches up with a caravan while it is in a deep valley, men and camels are in trouble. The camels sink in the wet sand. Since their leg bones are brittle and break easily, the camelmen have to pull them through. Each rainfall is followed by swarms of insects and mosquitoes, which make life unbearable for man and beast. However, almost overnight after a rain, grass begins to sprout and there is water for drinking.

Insects infest the camels' hides, causing swellings and sores. Birds like to perch on their backs as they rest, to feast on the insects. At the same time the birds dig their bills deeper into the poor animals' hides. Camelmen care for these sores by applying camel dung to the wounds to cool and help dry them.

It is hard to say which is worse: an insect-infested camp, where neither man nor beast can have a few hours of much-needed rest and sleep, but where there is ample water and pasture, or a caved-in or dried-up well, which the guide has used only a few weeks before. Sometimes men and camels have to await their turn at a well for as long as five hours, because a nearby well has caved in or been choked with windblown sand, and the remaining well must serve many more travelers and animals.

Finally, if all goes well, the caravan travels on at its even, calm pace. The camels follow one another in single files. Sometimes the camelmen can relax. The driver pulls the neck of a camel down, climbs up, and seats himself in front of the load. He slips off his large sandals and rests his tired feet against the camel's neck. He may even shut his eyes for a quick nap.

The loads of early caravans consisted of rugs,

cotton cloth, embroidered cloth, silks, silver, gold, mirrors, jewelry, perfumes, ivory, hides and worked leather goods, tools and needles, metals, ostrich skins, feathers, spices, kola nuts, live parrots, precious woods, sheets of tin and copper.

Caravans can carry everything. To the Tuareg, they bring the essentials—tea, sugar, salt, tobacco, grain, dates, cloth, various household furnishings, weapons, and ammunition. The Sahara's most important product is salt. Salt is as important to people as water. Without it, as without water, there can be no life. In fact, many scientists claim that great civilizations have developed in regions where there was an abundant and steady supply of salt. The civilizations collapsed when salt became unobtainable. The Sahara, fortunately, has ample salt deposits, and the salt has been carried by caravans to its neighbors for thousands of years. Some of these salt caravans are under Tuareg control, and are their main source of wealth.

The caravan routes over the Sahara connect with the three most important rock-salt deposits: Taoudéni, Bilma, and Demi. In numerous other places people can get salt locally. The rock salt of

Taoudéni is excellent. It is white and dense. Even in North Africa, where salt from European sources is shipped in, the housewife still prefers to buy the Taoudéni salt, brought in by caravan. The miners of Taoudéni, which is absolute desert, depend on the outside for all their needs: tobacco, sugar, tea, grain, dried meats, cheese, fats. Caravans, loaded with supplies for the miners, leave twice a year—in March and November—from Timbuctoo, which is the main trading center for the Taoudéni salt. It takes the caravan three weeks to get from Timbuctoo to Taoudéni. If supplies do not arrive in time, the miners may die of starvation. Some years ago a caravan with supplies for these miners was late. When it finally reached Taoudéni, many of the miners were dead.

The miners were mostly slaves. In the old days they had to work at Taoudéni, year after year, in heat and salt water. Now these miners can return to Timbuctoo and to their families from time to time, to enjoy their earnings for a while. If nothing better turns up, they again volunteer for the salt mines.

Nowadays, Arab youths, also, anxious to earn money, go away for a few months to dig salt, too. They stack the large salt slabs, tied with rope, so they will be ready for the camels. A slab of salt weighs about fifty pounds. The miners receive the equivalent of twenty-five cents per slab. Some of the payment is made in food and trade goods.

The camels are loaded with the salt, and start on their journey back to Timbuctoo. At Timbuctoo shippers wait to buy the salt. They pay as much as a dollar and a half per slab, or three cents a pound. In turn, these shippers make a large profit selling the salt at African coastal ports and at towns up the Niger River.

After the camels in the caravan have rested up, they are again loaded and join other caravans going north and east. But, come November, the camels will again leave Timbuctoo for Taoudéni in another salt caravan. At least 100,000 camel loads of salt are still shipped annually from Taoudéni alone.

Bilma, in eastern Niger, has the finest salt de-

posits in Africa. The salt, which is pink, is mined as in Taoudéni, and distributed north and south and into East Africa. The Tuareg noblemen get most of the profit from the sale of this salt and from the other goods in the caravans that carry it. In October small camel caravans from all over the Sahara begin their journey toward Bilma. They stop at trading centers and dispose of the trade goods they carry—especially dates, which grow in the northern Saharan oases—and buy goods to carry to Bilma.

Out of Bilma, loaded with salt, the caravans again disperse along various Saharan routes, to sell their salt and any other trade goods from small caravans that have joined up along the way. The

men then return home for a rest. Pack camels, under the charge of herders, are sent off to pastures to fatten up and rest too. In a few weeks men and camels will be plying the gravelly routes of the Sahara once again.

At one time the Tuareg controlled all the caravan routes in their lands. Only caravans that paid tribute to the chief of each territory they passed through were safe. From time to time, large caravans tried to get through Tuareg territories on their own, carrying their own guides and armed men. But the Tuareg invariably caught up with them and raided them. Eventually it became clear to the caravan owners that it paid to have Tuareg protection, not only in Tuareg homelands, but sometimes elsewhere in the Sahara as well, since raiders from other tribes feared the Tuareg.

Raiders usually arrived and escaped over the least-traveled routes, over barren, rough land where water was hard to get, to make sure the owners of the caravans would hesitate about following them. But each raider had to be on the lookout constantly.

Formerly small groups of Tuareg warriors raided other Tuareg camps and caravans. They attacked at dawn and forced the surprised shepherds to drive away their camels and flocks of sheep and goats. Some distance from the camp the raiders divided the herders and the booty among themselves. Each raider then took charge of his share and drove to his camp. The raided animals mingled with his stock, and the shepherds continued herding under their new masters.

A captured herder was treated well, and so had no reason to return to his old master, although he missed his family. Besides, since raiders usually attacked camps that were about 100 miles or more away from their own home base, a poor shepherd hardly dared to venture into the desert that far alone. He did not know the way or the location of water in the strange land.

However, no one in the Sahara remains isolated for long. Eventually someone noticed the brands on the stolen flock and reported them to the former owner, who organized a raid in return.

The code of desert raiding was to try never to burn a home or to kill anyone. To kill invited revenge, which led to blood feuds. An entire tribe was ready to fight in such a blood feud, and so a war between Tuareg tribes would arise. However, to kill in battle was an accepted part of warfare.

When opposing sides tired sufficiently of warring and raids, their chiefs met in council to make peace. A Tuareg nobleman acted as mediator. Payment to the injured parties could be made in livestock and services. The amount of this blood payment depended on the status of the persons who were killed. It often took years for a clan to pay a blood debt. Some clans got so deep into debt they became vassals of a noble clan, which had loaned them money or animals to pay their debts.

Tuareg raids have not been conducted on a

large scale in modern times, but accounts of past raids and wars make exciting stories to men resting in the evening after a day on the road. A storyteller always has ready listeners among the camelmen, and together they relive famous exploits.

FIVE

THE OASIS

The network of caravan routes that have developed through the Sahara has been determined by oases. An oasis is a place in the desert where water has been made available—a green place in the buff and black wasteland.

Small traveling units, such as nomads covering short distances, know where they can get enough water for their camps and their herds at a spring or a well. But a large caravan of hundreds of camels and a hundred or more men is hard put to get enough water and fodder, unless it camps near an oasis. Also, camelmen can carry only a limited supply of food. For long journeys that take a month or two, men and animals have to get supplies from a trading center at an oasis.

The large oases of the Sahara, especially the ones in the north where there are thousands of date palms, are entirely the work of men. The soil in the oases is no different from the soil in the rest of the Sahara. But with water, fertilizer, and human labor, the desert has been made to bloom. The low areas, where water can be drawn from wells for irrigation, are reserved for palm groves, orchards, and gardens. Higher up, in the more arid sections that cannot be made productive, people build houses of adobe and stone. To protect themselves against desert winds, sand, and raiders, the people surround each cluster of houses with a red clay wall.

The distant ancestors of the oases farmers must have crowded into these small areas when the Saharan rainfall began to decrease about four thousand years ago. Their descendants learned how to cultivate and irrigate the available land. They not only survived, but succeeded in turning their settlements into havens and trading centers for outsiders.

The original inhabitants of the Sahara, the Negroid peoples, are still in the majority today in these oases. They are the farmers. The traders and storekeepers have come in from the outside. Some are Berbers, some are Arabs, and some are Asians. There has been much mixing of people and much intermarriage among these groups throughout the centuries. The Tuareg also inter-married occasionally with their slaves and serfs and with Berbers of other tribes as well as Arabs.

On the northern edge of Tuareg territory a special group of slaves worked as skilled well diggers. They knew how to build the system of wells, called foggaras, that assured the farmers of a slow but steady water supply, which was used to irrigate considerable areas.

There is a water table everywhere under the soil. Recently a French geologist, Justin Savornin, who had been studying the geology of the Sahara, discovered water-bearing sandstone layers, deep underground. Today everyone in the Sahara knows of these layers, which have been dubbed the Alb, short for Albion. The water found in the Alb strata is now called Savornin's Sea, in honor of its discoverer. This sandy, water-bearing layer varies in thickness from 300 to over 1000 feet. When wells are sunk into it, water gushes forth.

As long as the people of the Sahara, whether Africans or Europeans, have water they do not care if it is slightly salty and not entirely clear. The water from Savornin's Sea is just that. It is also very old, because the water in the Alb strata collects very slowly, through gravity seepage. It is estimated that the rainwater shed over the Atlas mountains takes something like a century to reach Savornin's Sea as it seeps down underground and southward into the Sahara.

In the old days of the foggaras, when wells were dug by hand, the wells were at most some forty fathoms in depth. This is about 240 feet. A fathom is a measure of six feet. It is the width of a man's extended arms from fingertips to fingertips. An experienced well digger found the place where the water was at its highest level for that region. At this point he and his helpers dug a well. Nearby they dug shafts, twenty to fifty feet apart, in a downhill direction from the well. The shafts slanted toward the gardens and the orchards. The men then connected, via tunnels, the well with the shafts and let the water flow slowly down them. Little water was wasted by this method, for the tunnels were deep enough to prevent much evaporation. It all flowed slowly from the shafts into the irrigation ditches of the small garden plots in the oases. At one time these systems of foggaras existed in oases all across the Sahara. In places, where water was available the year round, people built reservoirs as well as wells. Many foggaras are still in use today.

Some wells in the Sahara are masterpieces of engineering skill. They are perfect circles. Yet they were all dug by hand and sometimes lined with stone by hand. A well was dug with a short hoe. The men threw the earth into buckets, which their helpers lowered and pulled up with ropes. Sometimes, after a well was dug, a skilled stone-mason was let down deep inside it, clinging perhaps to a boulder in the wall of the well. As cut

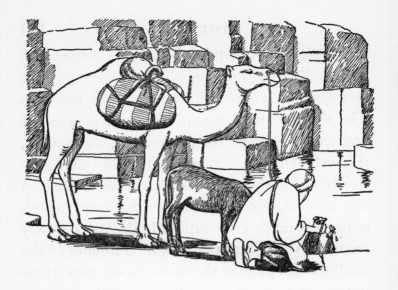

stones were lowered to him, he laid them inside the well walls, laboring day after day. There were, of course, inevitable accidents. Often a well claimed a life or a few lives in construction.

The men responsible for building a reservoir or for digging a well are considered the owners. Each farmer pays them for the use of their water. Water is usually measured by the number of minutes it is permitted to flow into a farmer's ditches.

Men in caravans carry their own leather buckets and ropes for raising water from wells. Camelmen makes ropes from sisal fibers during

their leisure evenings with the caravan. These ropes are also used as ties for camel packs, as camel lead ropes, and as bridles.

Since water is so vital, the people who live in a region near a well do not refuse to sell a caravan the water from it. But when a well is shallow or threatens to run dry, the people in that area may secretly cover it and hide it under brush and sand from strangers. A Targui guide, of course, knows all the wells, springs, and water holes on his route. When he finds a well covered, he will uncover it, provided he knows of no other well in the vicinity. After the caravan has taken the water it needs, the guide carefully covers the well again, to prevent it from becoming choked with sand. To willfully destroy a well is the greatest crime in the desert.

In some oases and cities in the south and where wells are not deep, people get water by using a very long pole, mounted in the middle of a forked post. A long rope and bucket hang down from the top end of the pole, while a boulder weighs down the other end. The contraption works like a seesaw. When a person pulls on the rope, the pole swings down, lowering the bucket into the well. When the bucket is filled with water, he loosens his hold on the rope. The weight swings the opposite end of the pole down to ground level. The person lightly guides the rope so the filled bucket does not swing too much and spill water.

Gardening in the oases is done by hand and hoe, since the plots are only about six feet square. Even if they could use plows, the farmers could hardly afford to buy them. Each six-foot patch is surrounded by an irrigation channel, which connects with the main irrigation ditch.

When water for the fields comes from a deep well or a reservoir, a man and an old camel work all day long to fill the irrigation ditches. The camel, tied to a rope and pulley, pulls a leather bucket from the well to the irrigation ditch and then returns to repeat the process. The leather bucket is so constructed that its bottom opens when a cord is pulled.

When a farmer knows he has enough water, he hoes the garden and plants his seed. Then he spreads manure and turns it under. In the Saharan oases the farmers can grow two or more crops a year because of the warm climate and because of this intensive cultivation. The crops are millet, guinea corn, onions, tomatoes, beans, pumpkins, watermelons, carrots, turnips, spinach, sweet potatoes. Sometimes they also grow a little cotton for making thread and cord. These farmers buy most of their cloth from traders.

Years ago the serfs in the oases depended on the Tuareg warriors to protect them against raiders. They never were completely secure, however, since a full hut, with harvested grain and produce, was a temptation to marauders. After the harvest, farmers spoke among themselves about raids and listened to rumors. A villager might have seen a group of men on camels. They looked suspicious, and he hurried with the news to the village. To cheer themselves, the men repeated the saying that worry was for cowards. But they worried all the same.

The farmers set aside the grain and produce intended for their nomad protectors in baskets and sacks to await collection. The collecting of farm produce is an established procedure. A farmer may have worked an extra piece of land, and so has a bigger harvest, which he has to share with the owner. In turn, the collector has to meet his own obligations. If the share of the harvests he collects from the farmers proves insufficient for his household, he may demand more. If the harvest has been good, his terms will be easier. But each farmer knows by this time the habits and attitudes of the men who will come to collect. He and his sons expect that the collector will thoroughly look over and search their home and storage huts, to make sure they have been fair and have not kept more than their share. There is no way, however, for the collector to ascertain exactly how big the harvest was, so the farmers can cautiously set aside a bit more for themselves and a bit less for the tribute.

In the larger northern oases, more fruits and vegetables are grown. The farmers there also enjoy more than one crop a year. The date palms, however, produce only one crop, but they are the most important crop. Date palms grow not only in the northern half of the Sahara, but on the Mediterranean coast up to altitudes of 2500 feet. The palms are native to both North Africa and Arabia, and have been cultivated since ancient times. Dates to the Saharans are like maize, or corn, to the American Indians, and rice to the peoples of Asia. They are the "bread" of the desert region north of the Tropic of Cancer. In the southern Sahara, where dates are brought in by caravan, they are too expensive for the poorer people.

Date palms grow to a hundred foot height. They begin to bear fruit after ten years. With care, they continue bearing fruit for perhaps as much as a hundred years or more. The date palm

has been exported to the warmer regions of the United States and to Central America, and can be seen in botanical gardens. A ripe date is about an inch and a half to two inches long, yellowish or reddish brown, meaty and sweet. Only the female trees bear fruit, so a grower permits no more than a few male palms in each grove. Depending on its age, a date palm bears between 40 and 170 pounds of dates annually.

The date palms are sometimes tapped, as we tap maple trees, although tapping is not good for the palms and will eventually kill them. Like maple sap, if palm juice is allowed to evaporate, it turns into palm sugar. The juice tastes, they say, like coconut milk. When it ferments, it turns into a strong, smelly alcoholic drink.

Since date palms grow so tall, the fruit growers plant apricots, pomegranates, grapefruit, oranges, lemons, and peaches in their shade. They plant some garden crops in the groves, too, and fig trees just outside the groves. The palm groves need regular watering—usually every ten days or so. A palm tree can withstand a dry period, but it will yield no fruit. Some palm trees have been planted to a depth of several feet, where there is an underground stream. However, they cannot tolerate stagnant water.

Palm groves are owned by noblemen and vassals. When the crop is weighed, the households of the owners receive their share of the dates as well as other fruit. The serfs and slaves are also paid in dates.

Dates were the main article of trade and the greatest source of income for the northern fruit growers. They took the choicest dates to market and sold them for immediate consumption, since ripe dates do not keep for long. Other dates were stuffed into goatskins, pressed, and made into a marmalade. The remaining crop was pressed into long thick bricks. These pressed-date bricks kept for a longer time, and could be transported easily. Oasis tradesmen bought up quantities of them and sold them in turn to incoming caravans.

In the past the northern oases attracted large caravans, and the tradesmen enjoyed great wealth. They built fine two- or three-story homes and mosques. The poorer people in both the northern and southern oases lived in small huts of adobe; in the south they also lived in *zeribas*.

Craftsmen like to live in towns to cater to the tradesmen, farmers, and visitors. Of the crafts-men, the smiths are the most skillful. The Tua-reg call them Inaden. They avoid contact with them, but depend on them. For some reason, throughout the Tuareg world, as well as elsewhere in Africa, the smiths are held in low esteem. They live by themselves on the outskirts of towns or camps in the poorest hovels or *zeribas*.

Using a simple anvil and a goatskin bellows, with a pair of wooden slats and an iron nozzle, a smith melts down silver coins and makes jewelry for the Tuareg women. They make iron adzes, hammers, files, chisels, and shears. The knives they make are as good as European knives. From time to time a smith will set up his simple anvil in a Tuareg camp, fill their orders, mend some tools, and depart.

In the southern Sahara the Inaden women also tan leather. Some of the handsome sword sheaths are made by these people. With the simplest tools, an Inaden also turns out beautiful, thin-walled wooden bowls, ladles, and spoons needed in a Tuareg household. Today the status of the Inaden is rising, and greater respect is being shown their skill. Tourists are glad to pay high prices for their products.

Trading in the small stalls of towns and in the marketplace is noisy. Traders shout bargains at the top of their voices in order to attract buyers. Haggling over prices marks every sale. The seller tries to get the highest price. The buyer tries to pay the lowest price. Each knows it. Since there is no set price for anything, the seller begins by

asking an exorbitant price. He expects the buyer
to offer him much less. They bargain and argue.
Each proclaims his honesty to the other. Also his
poverty. And each, of course, distrusts the other.
Yet tradesmen respect good bargainers. A man
who pays a price without bargaining is considered
a fool.

Transactions in salt and grain are measured by
the camel load, but these camel loads are never
the same twice. The actual weights and measures
are known to the town official, but he is not expected to be any more honest than the tradesmen.

In packing salt for loading, the owners will slip in inferior salt blocks, cover them with good ones, and sell each load with loud proclamations that it holds the finest salt mined that year. Into bundles of produce and vegetables, the tradesmen slip some spoiled stuff. They might mix sand with their grain. It is impossible for the buyer to check all of the loads. He may be able to examine a few —always over the noisy protests of the seller, whose feelings are hurt because his honesty is questioned.

A unit of measure is a handful with the five fingers closed. Six such handfuls make a *tefakint*, a small basket. In some places five of these baskets make a *muda*. In other places a *muda* is ten baskets. This, of course, leads to more arguments, more trading.

Cloth is measured by the *aghil* and *amitral*. An *aghil* is a length from the elbow to the tip of the middle finger. Ten such *aghils* equal one *amitral*.

Distance is measured in days or parts of a day. A Targui will say, "We are half a day from my camp." He means that, traveling at a speed of about twenty miles a day by camel, his camp is ten miles away. On ground too rough to keep up a normal pace, a camel will cover only ten miles a day.

Today the tradesmen use money. In the old days they used cowrie shells by the thousand. They used gold, too, but it was not as easy to handle. The Maria Theresa dollar, a silver coin minted in Austria, was also used. Dated 1780, it bore the image of Maria Theresa of Austria. Through trade it spread throughout the East and soon came to be called the Levant dollar. Its present worth is less than fifty cents in United States currency. With French occupation of the Sahara, French francs, mostly silver coins, have come more and more into use, displacing all other currency in Saharan trading. But the Tuareg still rely less on currency than on trading one article for another.

No marketplace is ever without its crowd of men and camels, sheep and goats. Men may come to sell produce and linger in the marketplace, looking over a camel that is offered at a good price. Or several men may join in buying a camel.

All now bargain noisily. In the days when camels were raided regularly, stolen camels might be driven to a faraway marketplace for a quick sale. The exhausted animals, badly in need of rest and fodder, could be purchased at a low price. There isn't a camelman born who can resist such a bargain, even if he does suspect that he is buying a stolen animal.

Animals can be pastured in valleys near the oases. The farmers need goats for milk and cheese, and for meat from time to time. In the north the hairy sheep are also milked. A donkey is handy to carry loads. Livestock, therefore, is continuously traded, bought, and sold.

As men trade and talk, they also learn. Trading towns have been called great civilizers. When trading is completed, each party, sure that he has bested the other, can now retire into a stall for a steaming glass of sweet tea and talk. The hot noon is thus spent in the pleasant exchange of ideas and family histories, in discussions of customs and of men's needs, and in stories and jokes in general. World events are rarely spoken of. Instead they discuss the weather, recent caravan news, poverty, and riches. A holy man may join a group and speak of his experiences, of his beliefs, and of the future of man. The conversation gives the listeners much food for thought during the long days riding in a caravan or tending their groves and gardens. New ideas are mulled over and accepted or rejected. Thus changes begin to take place in jobs, in varieties of foods, in clothes, in household furnishings, and in people's thinking and ways.

SIX

RELIGION AND CEREMONIES

The Tuareg, it is said, are not religious. The Koran, the Bible of the Moslems, prescribes that men pray five times a day. Most Tuareg pray only once a day. Some do not pray at all. The Moslems believe in one god, Allah. Mohammed was Allah's spokesman and messenger. The Koran is the book of laws for the Moslem religion, which is called Islam. The Moslem house of worship is a mosque. In it men and women worship separately.

Most Moslems, except for the Tuareg, believe women are inferior to men. Therefore, they do not permit them to worship with men.

In the towns people pray wherever they happen to be—at home, in the open field, or in a shop. When prayer time comes—at dawn, at noon, in the midafternoon, at dusk, after dark—a man quickly spreads out a mat, removes his shoes, washes his hands and feet, covers his head, and kneels on the mat to pray. Before the Tuareg pray, they "wash" their hands by rubbing them in the hot desert sand, since they have so little water to spare for washing. The prayer is simple and silent. A praying Moslem seems deeply ab-

sorbed with his inner self. One feels that he is in communion with his God.

The Tuareg camps have no mosques. But here and there a rectangle of small stones is laid out— a small space where men come to pray. The stones are always left in place. Other Tuareg who camp there later will recognize the place as one where the Kel Tagilmus, the People of the Veil, prayed to Allah. It will be respected and held sacred. No Moslem will hesitate to pray there.

Both *Moslem* and *Islam* are Arabic words. Islam means "submitting" to God. A Moslem is a person who submits. Mohammed taught Islamic beliefs to the Arabs in their original homeland on the Arabian Peninsula. Mohammed was born there, in Mecca. The date of his birth is not certain. It is believed he was born sometime in 570 A.D. Mohammed died in 632, at about the age of sixty-two. The date of his death *is* certain.

Mohammed was a wealthy merchant. Early in the seventh century Mohammed had a dream in which he was instructed to preach religion as he understood it. But the people of his city, Mecca, evidently refused to accept the new reli-

gion. Mohammed had to move north from Mecca
to Medina, where he continued preaching and
gained followers. The time of his move to Medina
and the date of the birth of Islam are given as the
year 622. Mohammed was, according to scholars,
a great and inspired man. His preachings and
revelations are recorded in the Koran. Men who
devote years to studying the Koran are considered
holy men.

The Moslem calendar has only 354 days. For
every 33 years of the Moslem calendar, the Christian calendar has only 32 years. The most important month in Islam, Ramadan, is their ninth
month—and it is a period of fasting. The birth
of Mohammed and the end of the Moslem year
are also important festivals, as are Christmas and
New Year's Day to us.

Wherever they went, Arabian merchants and
holy men preached their new religion. Some went
to Egypt; some to the rest of East Africa; some
into Asia and, later, into Europe. In the seventh
century the Arabs began the conquest of North
Africa. During that and the following centuries
Islam began to be established among the peoples

of the Sahara. Many accepted the religion, because they were moved by the teachings of Mohammed. Others *had* to become Moslems, because they were conquered and Islam was forced upon them. There are no details as to how the Tuareg tribes were converted. However, although they took on Islam, the Tuareg held to many of their former beliefs.

The Tuareg have their own tribal chiefs, who also act as judges. But there have been one or two occasions, when groups, feuding among themselves, asked a holy man to step in as an impartial judge and the opposing sides accepted his judgment. Because the tribal chiefs were involved in the dispute, it seemed best for an outsider to settle matters. A holy man's decision is all the more respected, because his judgment will be upheld by Allah.

For services performed, the Arab holy men receive gifts, which support them and their disciples. Since the Tuareg are firm believers in charms to ward off all kinds of evil and to bring the wearers good luck, holy men collect additional fees and gifts for the charms they prepare. A charm is usually a specially inscribed piece of paper or parchment, or a metal tag for a camel. The inscription is a sentence or a prayer from the Koran. The holy man writes it down and gives it away on special occasions. Women make tiny decorated leather pouches for the charms. The smiths make tiny silver boxes for them. After a charm is placed in its pouch or box, it will be worn on a handsome plaited leather string, and its wearer will never part with it.

A boy gets his first charm before his naming ceremony. Several years later, after he is circumcised, other charms may be sold to him by a holy man. Still later, following his initiation into manhood, when a boy gets his first sword, a holy man who is present at the festival may also sell him a charm. When the young man has reached adulthood and is presented with a veil, which he will wear for the rest of his life, he may receive still more charms. All these charms are worn together. Some men wear dozens of them, like multistringed necklaces. In the life of danger the Tuareg lead, such charms are comforting, and a man welcomes the extra power they give him for emergencies.

To this collection of charms men add others of their own choice. Some they may have inherited. Others, found in the desert, seem to the Tuareg symbols of strength, such as the head and beak of a hawk, a specially shaped piece of bone, or an attractive sand-polished stone. They are added for good measure to the charms a person already has. Some men sew charms into their cloaks and *gondouras*, or tuck them in their veils to prevent headaches, soreness of the eyes, nosebleeds, and earaches.

Charms guard the wearer against evil spirits and sorcery. They guard a person against enemy bullets, help a man escape from his enemies, and assist him in successful trading. A woman believes that charms make pregnancies and births easier. A charm will help keep her baby well and her husband unharmed.

Belief in the words of the Koran is strong. A holy man might inscribe a passage from the Koran in charcoal, then wash off the inscription, and have a patient drink the potion. If such a mixture of charcoal and water is given a patient three times, he will be cured. The holy man can sometimes cure the sick by his very presence. Often he spits on his palms while reciting a passage from the Koran, and then rubs them over the face of the patient to cure him.

Farmers in oases invite a holy man to visit them at planting time. The holy man recites a passage from the Koran and spits into sand. This sand is then sprinkled over the gardens to keep mice and insects out.

If the harvest is a poor one, or if a holy man fails to cure a patient, no one blames him. He simply says, "Allah did not will it so." The people agree and say, "It was not the will of Allah."

Holy men attend most family celebrations in the oases, such as marriages and births, naming, circumcision, and initiation ceremonies. They are also present when people are sick, when they die, and when they are buried.

The Tuareg, like most people, believe in an afterlife. On Judgment Day all the dead will come to life. A person's breath is the life within him. When he is about to die, spirits appear and take away his breath. Relatives come at once to wrap the body in cloth and in mats for burial.

The body is buried nearby, and the people immediately pack up and move away to another camp.

A man takes his shadow with him when he dies. The image of a dead person, however, has the magic to leave the grave and wander about on earth long after his death, visiting relatives and friends. It may do harm, and seldom any good. The image is curious about what is happening to its family. It is happy to hear prayers of relatives. It likes to hear what people say about it, and enters their homes after they are asleep to listen to their dreams. That is why people dream of the dead. A mother who has lost a child sometimes sleeps on its grave. During the night the baby's image visits her. She says in the morning that she has dreamed of her loved one.

The Tuareg believe spirits live in the heavens, underground, and in the desert. They come out at night to play. Noises one hears in the desert at night are the spirits talking. In camps, women put out small bowls of cereal and millet for these spirits to eat. They usually find the bowls empty and clean in the morning.

Outdoor men like the Tuareg watch the earth, sky, sun, and stars all the time. They know a great deal about weather forecasting. However, some of this forecasting is mingled with fears and forebodings. Some think that a rainbow is a sign of rain. That is a good omen, of course, but men will be careful not to camp in a low place where they will be flooded out. A rainbow in the morning is considered a bad sign. About fifty years ago World War I brought fighting into the Sahara. A rainbow was seen then in the early morning. Now people firmly believe that it brings evil, wars, and raids. A wind from the northwest bodes no good. It usually brings a haze and a sandstorm and perhaps raiders from the north. People watch clouds. If the air is very still and the clouds float overhead like thick white cotton, people fear that something evil will happen. When, at sunset, a deep cloud on the horizon swallows the sun, it is also believed to be evil.

The Tuareg do not eat the foods that the Koran forbids Moslems to eat. Among the Tuareg food taboos are pork, chicken, eggs, and dog, horse, and donkey meat. The Tuareg claim these ani-

mals are unclean. Yet, when hungry, they will eat
rats and mice. But they do not eat jerboas, tiny
kangaroolike creatures of the desert. The Tuareg
say they are as unclean as pigs. They also say that
eating fish, birds, and big lizards has been for-
bidden to them. The Tuareg believe the big lizards are among their ancient ancestors and, like
American Indian totems, must not be killed or
eaten.

However, the hairy sheep is very acceptable as
a sacrifice to Allah, because it is so rare. This custom of sacrificing an animal in thanksgiving is
common among the Tuareg. On reaching home
after a long caravan journey, a chief sometimes
orders that a goat be brought to him. He then
sacrifices it as an offering of thanks for having
come home safely. When there is sickness among
the camels and all remedies seem to fail, a nobleman may select a goat or two and sacrifice them,
with a prayer that his camels may recover.

The important fast of Ramadan is observed by
very few Tuareg in the Sahara. However, the end
of this fast is followed by three days of celebration
and feasting, called the Feast of the Sheep, and

many Tuareg come to the city to see the celebration.

On the first day of the Feast of the Sheep, in the city of Agades (a-gah-des') in the Air (ah-ehr'), the entire population turns out to celebrate the start of the feast. In the early morning everyone in town—men, women, children, visiting traders, and camelmen—begins the trek from the city itself and from surrounding camps to the outskirts of Agades. Every Tuareg who owns a camel or can borrow one arrives proudly seated on his mount. The men, dressed in their very best indigo *gondouras*, wear all the silver ornaments they own or can borrow from friends. Some tie a red cloth over the dark veils. Some vassal Tuareg wear white robes. All carry their swords with the crosslike hilts. Some even carry spears.

The colorful throng awaits the arrival of the sultan of Agades and the head of the noble Kel Owi tribes. These dignitaries ride handsome white camels. They line up facing the gathering. The sultan and his officers are dressed in white. The Kel Owi chief wears the usual indigo *gondoura*, but there is a touch of white on his veil.

Their armed bodyguard, also riding camels, lines up behind them.

The Feast of the Sheep begins with a prayer. Everyone dismounts. The people prostrate themselves. The sultan and the chief of the Kel Owi do the same. The only figure that remains standing close to the sultan is a single warrior of the Tuareg bodyguard. He stands tall in his indigo robe and veil, with his naked sword pointed to the ground, his arm resting on his cross hilt. The remaining bodyguards, their swords drawn, raise them each time the sultan bows in prayer.

The prayer ends. Everyone rises and remains standing. Two sheep are brought in. One of the sultan's officers pulls out his knife and slits their throats. Men rush forward and wash off the spilled blood before it dries.

Solemnly the men mount their camels. The crowd, after this final cleansing of their sins through sacrifice, happily turns back to the city for a three-day holiday of feasting and merry-making.

SEVEN

THE TUAREG TODAY

The government the Tuareg developed had its origins among their Berber ancestors. The Berbers governed themselves as independent tribal units, and the Tuareg preserved the same independence.

Each clan—whether nobles or vassals—selects its own clan chief. In camps the spokesman is head of his family. When several families are involved, the most respected nobleman becomes the spokesman. The serfs, in their villages, also have their local elected government and chiefs. Men select their tribal chiefs and clan chiefs, and vote for them in councils. A chief can be deposed, if the heads of families feel he is not doing his job or is not a good judge.

Even though Tuareg women are held in high esteem and the chief is selected because of his mother's clan, women do not have a vote. When a chief dies, another is chosen. The new chief need not be a close relative of the deceased chief, although he may be from the same clan. The men usually vote for the best man.

Imrad, or vassal, chiefs sit in tribal councils with the Imochar, or noble, chiefs, but the Imrad usually obey Imochar decisions. However, the noblemen do not order the vassals about. When a nobleman wishes the services and help of a vassal, he speaks to his noble clan chief, who, in turn, speaks to the vassal clan chief. If an Imrad family is not happy living in the camp of one Imochar, they can move away to another camp, where they hope their relations with the noblemen will be better. But although the Imrad may change from one camp to another, they cannot leave the noble tribe, and probably would not even wish it. Some of the Imrad clans are rich. They are respected, and enjoy the services of their serfs. They do not suffer from the pride of the nobles, who feel that manual labor is beneath them. Imrad are not quite as unwilling to work with their hands. Sometimes they manage the herds and flocks for the Imochar. They oversee their groves and gardens. For all of these jobs the Imrad receive a share of the produce.

Tuareg slaves and herders obeyed the Imochar or Imrad chief of the household in which they worked. However, if a slave was unhappy with his lot, he could not leave his master.

When a tribe gets too large and begins to spread out, it may eventually split in two. One retains the original name. The other, also made up of nobles, vassals, and serfs, keeps the name Kel and adds to it the name of the place where the newly formed tribe is centered.

Today the Saharan Tuareg are divided into four confederacies—the Ajjer; the Ahaggar; the Adrar-n-Iforas, a division of the Ahaggar; and the Air. A confederacy is a self-governing group of several noble clans and vassal clans, their serfs, and other dependents. Each confederation has its own territory. Each gets its name from that territory.

Water, pasture, and land for farming are available in all four regions. The Tuareg still raise camels, hairy sheep, goats, donkeys, and cattle. The farmers raise millet, barley, onions, gourds, melons, and a little wheat. They have small groves of fruit trees. Dates are still harvested annually in small eastern and western oases.

None of these confederacies, however, is entirely self-sufficient. The Tuareg need a great many things from the outside: cloth, tea, sugar, metals, and household goods. These items call for a larger income than the Tuareg earn from their flocks, their camels, and their dates. The farmers do not produce enough to export farm products. However, the salt caravans are still profitable and are the largest source of income for the people.

The pattern of Tuareg life today is determined by the seasons. In spring and fall the Imochar and Imrad camp together in tents and live off the products of their herds and camels. In summer they camp in *zeribas* and consume the produce of the farms. The highlands are cooler and more comfortable at this time of year. In winter the men go out with their caravans. Under the French government, some joined the Camel Corps, to aid caravans and help police the desert.

Today the tribes of each confederacy live within their own territory, and are self-governing. A tribe is made up of one or more noble clans, several vassal clans, freed serfs, and the descendants of slaves. A noble clan, such as the Kel Rela in Ahaggar, gives its name to its entire tribe. The names of the other clans in the tribe will also begin with the word *Kel* (meaning people), but the second name will be different. From among the Kel Rela is selected the chief for the entire Ahaggar confederation. This chief of the Ahaggar Tuareg is called the *amenokal*. He is a leader in war and a judge in peacetime. He presides at the councils, and has authority over the Imrad clans that are associated with his confederation.

The Air Confederacy is made up of the Kel Owi

tribes and the five tribes of the People of the King. The Kel Owis, the most recent people to come into the Sahara, arrived around 1740. They have been influenced by living close to Arabs and Sudanese people. The five tribes of the People of the King are the ancient settled farmers of the Air. The Air Confederacy is ruled jointly by a chief whom the Kel Owi tribes select and by the *amenokal* of the People of the King. The Kel Owis' chief is a noble, whose title is *anastafidet*. An *anastafidet* is chosen from one of two noble Kel Owi tribes, and holds office for three years. He lives in Agades, the capital of the Air Tuareg. His principal job is to maintain commercial contact with the numerous caravans that come to the Air.

The People of the King do not *elect* their *amenokal*, whom they also call Sultan or Amrar. His office is hereditary. The sultans of the Air are Negroes, as are the freed serf farmers of the Air. Legend has it that the people of the Air once sent a delegation to Constantinople, Turkey, to ask the caliph, the Moslem Commander of the Faithful, to send a prince to govern them. The delegation was kept waiting for three years, while the caliph made up his mind. None of his wives would consent to let one of their sons travel that far away from home. Finally, the caliph ordered that the son of one of his bodyguards be taken to the Air with his mother and some of her relatives. Ever since, the sultan has been a Negro, a descendant of the son of the caliph's bodyguard.

The sultan looks out for the People of the King. He, too, lives in Agades. He has a minister, or vizier, who is usually a noble Tuareg, to help him in foreign affairs. The vizier goes along with the salt caravans to Bilma, and he collects a tribute of one eighth of the salt mined. He also welcomes Arab traders who come to the Air. The Arabs call him Sheik el Arab, meaning Chief of the Arabs.

In addition, the sultan has another officer, a chief of the marketplace. He collects market dues and supervises the police and other officials. He watches over weights and measures, and tries to make sure foreign traders are treated fairly.

The slave trade, which was probably begun by

the Romans, continued with renewed vigor under Arab conquests. The profits from it were enormous. The Arab merchants had no qualms about whether slavery was right or wrong, since Moslems do not believe in equality among human beings. Arab traders accepted slaves from the interior, and paid for them in trade goods—swords, beads, and other luxuries—that were appreciated by the rulers of Africa's interior. These captives made the long journey on foot to the coast, where they were turned over to Arab merchants and shipped east and west. With the discovery of the New World, slaves were shipped to the West Indies and the Americas.

The Tuareg were never slave traders, although they captured slaves in raids for their own households. Rather, they were middlemen of the slave traffic up and down the Sahara. They did not try to compete with the slave merchants, but merely guided slave caravans to their destinations. From time to time, when a Targui guide liked the looks of a slave and thought he would make a good herder, or thought a woman would make an obedient and strong household slave, he traded for him or her. The descendants of these slaves are still with the Tuareg, and consider themselves Tuareg today. Although the slaves were freed after the French occupation of the Sahara, they remained in the service of their masters, and the Tuareg still look upon them as slaves.

In 1859 a Frenchman, Henri Duveyrier, explored the route from Ghat to Murzuk, and wrote a book about his travels, entitled *The Tuareg of the North*, which was published in France in 1864. Others who ventured deep into the interior of the Sahara were Eugene Joubert and R. Dourneaux-Dupere, in 1874. But both were killed on their return journey to Algeria. Still others traveled from Morocco to Timbuctoo, but skirted Tuareg territory. A few years later the Tuareg killed Colonel Paul Flatters, while he was surveying for the railroad to be built from Algeria south and west to Dakar, now the capital of Senegal.

Another famous traveler was the soldier, C. E. de Foucauld. De Foucauld disguised himself as a Jewish trader. At first he traveled in Morocco, but he turned to the Ahaggar, after meeting some Ahaggar Tuareg in Algeria. De Foucauld admired them, made friends with them, and for some thirty years lived as a missionary in the Ahaggar. Then in 1916 de Foucauld was murdered, and the Tuareg were blamed. The Tuareg kept asserting that de Foucauld had been their friend and that it is against Tuareg hospitality to kill a friend, even if he is a Frenchman. Later it was found that the murder had been accidental. The fact that de Foucauld succeeded in writing a dictionary of the Tamahek language proves that the Tuareg did like him enough to teach him Tamahek and to spend time helping him prepare his manuscript. The dictionary, entitled in French *Dictionnaire Touareg Français*, was published in Paris in 1952 in four volumes.

Scientific expeditions to the Sahara began early in the nineteenth century. Explorers studied and mapped the country. They spoke to Africans to learn more about them. They recorded rainfall, vegetation, and animal life. The most famous scientist was a German, Heinrich Barth, who later wrote a book, entitled *Travels and Discoveries in Northern and Central Africa*. Barth covered the country from Tripolitania to Lake Chad and across to Timbuctoo. He talked with the eastern and southern Tuareg, and studied them.

After 1870 a scramble began for the possession of African lands. European factories, created by the industrial revolution, needed raw materials, and Africa seemed a likely place to obtain them. Northwest Africa and the Sahara fell to France, which had already occupied Algeria in 1830. The French began to penetrate Tuareg territory seventy years later. They kept pushing south until they reached the Niger River. In all, after 1900, France controlled nearly the entire western half of the Sahara, except those west-coast states where Spain had established prior claims.

The French met with opposition, rebellion, and war, for the Africans preferred home rule. Eventually, however, the independent Tuareg, like the people of Morocco, Tunisia, and northern Algeria, found themselves subjects of France.

The first French governor of the Sahara was General Laperrine. He was in command of the northern oases, and his job was to take away the caravan routes in the Sahara from Tuareg control. In 1902 the Ahaggar Tuareg had a final battle with a French patrol of Arab camel riders, but were defeated because of the superior French arms. This defeat, however, did not stop raids against the French. The French then organized their now famous Camel Corps to patrol the desert. Not enough Frenchmen were skilled camel riders, so the French hired the Chaamba Arabs of the western Sahara. Armed with French rifles, the Chaamba, ancient enemies of the Tuareg, succeeded in subduing the people of the Ahaggar. In 1905, the Tuareg finally gave in and agreed to stop raiding.

General Laperrine then turned his attention to the Ajjer Tuareg. These tribes proved harder to subdue, for the Sanusi holy men of Tripolitania and a few Turkish camelmen joined with them against the French. Although it took a longer time, even the Ajjer had to give in, since neither they nor their allies could match European weapons.

During the First World War the Tuareg were incited by the Germans and Turks to rebel. Raids began once more. In 1917 the Tuareg of the Air revolted. A nobleman Tuareg, Kaossen, organized this last of the revolts. All the Air Tuareg joined him, including the Sultan of Agades, whose office is for peace, not war. Although the revolt was fanned by the Germans and Turks, the Tuareg saw it as an opportunity to rid the Air of the French, rather than a way to help Germany.

The fighting began when a group of corpsmen in the French Camel Corps started back to their fort near Agades after escorting a salt caravan to Bilma. They were only a day's journey away from Agades and suspected nothing, when a large gathering of Tuareg camelmen emerged from behind a hill and almost wiped out the entire platoon. Only one officer and a few Senegalese corpsmen escaped, and reached the fort at Agades. Here the entire French garrison was besieged, but it held out for three months, until help came from their army in Niger. Then the French garrison and their reinforcements turned full force against the Tuareg.

When this last revolt collapsed, the Tuareg ceased to try any large-scale hostility. Families gathered whatever food and possessions they could carry on their backs or on loaded donkeys, took

their few sheep and goats, and left their homes. They scattered mostly south and west, wherever they felt they would be safe. Fortunately not many perished. Those who wandered south found homes in Nigeria, where they were welcomed. Most have remained there ever since.

In 1922, five years after this forced exodus, the French issued a proclamation inviting the former residents to return home to the Air. Some did return.

An Englishman, Sir Francis Rennell Rodd, now Lord Rennell, visited the Air in 1922, and in his book, entitled *The People of the Veil*, he described the abandoned homes he visited. The weathered clay walls and roofs had caved in. Gardens that had been worked with such toil and care were now covered with sand. The camel herds of Agades were gone. In some of the homes valuable possessions, furniture, and household goods, now turning to dust, still lay where their owners had left them. It was a heartbreaking sight. The mosques had also caved in. No one cared to clean them up, since they had been desecrated by the French. No Moslem could pray in them again. He would rather use the open air and a circle of stones, and prostrate himself in the sand.

Noblemen, who returned to the Air without camels, sheep, or goats, began to till their gardens themselves. Sir Francis described one such nobleman, who later became his trusted friend and guide. They first met near the nobleman's hut. The Targui wore the traditional indigo veil, but his *gondoura* was in rags. On his feet were tattered sandals. His slender ankles, chapped and browned, had deep dents in them—the lifetime marks left by prison chains. He had been imprisoned in a French Saharan fort following the Tuareg revolt. But he still wore a handsome necklace of charms, and across his chest was a sword in a fine tooled-leather sheath. He had kept all that was of value to him of his noble heritage, including his dignity and pride.

The nobleman said, "I will come with you as your guide. I will come as soon as I have provided for my wife and son and after I have placed them safely in the hands of my relatives. Then I will

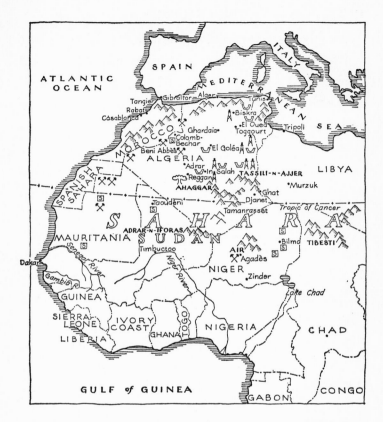

ATLANTIC
OCEAN

SPAIN

ITALY

MEDITERRANEAN

Tangier
Rabat
Casablanca
MOROCCO
Gibraltar
Alger
Tunis
Biskra
El Oued
Toggourt
Tripoli
SEA

Ghardaia
Colomb-
Bechar
Beni Abbès
El Goléa

ALGERIA
Adrar
In Salah
Reggan
AHAGGAR
TASSILI-N-AJJER
LIBYA

SPANISH SAHARA

Taoudeni
Ghat
Djanet
Tamanrasset
Murzuk
Tropic of Cancer

S A H A R A

ADRAR-N-IFORAS
SUDAN
MAURITANIA
Timbuctoo
AÏR
Agadès
Bilma
TIBESTI

Dakar
Senegal River
NIGER
Zinder

Gambia
Niger River
Lake Chad

GUINEA

SIERRA
LEONE
IVORY
COAST
GHANA
TOGO
NIGERIA
CHAD

LIBERIA

GULF of GUINEA

GABON
CONGO

WEST AFRICA TODAY

🌳 A-BOMB TESTING SITE   ✗ MINERALS

♠ OIL AND GAS WELLS   Ⓢ SALT MINES

Ⱳ ARTESIAN WELLS

MILES

0   200   400   600

come with you for a month or a year. But I come only because I want to come. Not for pay. When I come I will go anywhere you want, but not as your servant. I will not be paid for my services. You may give me a present if you like. You must feed me and give me a camel to ride, because I have none. But I will come only as your friend, because I myself wish to come."

There are boomtowns in the Tuareg Sahara today, as there are all over the desert. Oil, natural gas, and valuable mineral deposits were discovered in the Sahara after the Second World War. Now oil wells are being drilled everywhere. Drilling and well digging for water follow, since water is essential for men and machines. Today thousands of Saharans have ample water for the first time in their lives, and oases are being enlarged to accommodate the growing population. The Tuareg serfs and former slaves are very much in demand to help the crews of European technicians. By their former standards, the Africans are paid fabulous wages. As a result, a noble or vassal Targui often has to tend his own flocks and camels, because his help has deserted him for these better-paying jobs.

Today our hopes for the welfare and survival of the farmers in the oases are greater than they are for the nomadic Tuareg noblemen. The settled town people and the former serfs and slaves are more adaptable. They can face industrialization, and make the best of it. For the noblemen the future is not as bright. Motorized equipment is replacing the caravan. Whereas in the past the lifeblood of the Sahara was a camel and a goatskin filled with water, now it is the airplane and the air-conditioned desert truck. Bottled gas is used for refrigeration and the driver sits comfortably in an air-conditioned cab. The wheels alone of these supertrucks are some six feet high. Even a small five-ton truck, traveling over Saharan gravel, can cover over a hundred miles a day. It would take as many as 250 camels to carry as much, and they could cover only about a fifth of the distance in a day. Camels still carry oil to outlying airstrips, but one of the giant trucks can do the work of 5000 camels. Salt caravans still run and are still under Tuareg control, but the income from them is not enough to meet the Tuareg's increasing needs.

The entire Tuareg way of life, so carefully built up through the centuries to meet a harsh environment, is falling apart. The noblemen will not readily accept the modern changes forced upon them. And so they are the ones who are hurt the most by the winds of change that are now sweeping the Sahara and the rest of Africa.

INDEX

Indicates illustration

O

Oases, 34, 97–99, 104–110
  caravan trade, 110
  farming, 98–99, 104–105, 107–109
  housing, 98
  irrigation, 98–101, 104–105
  raids on, 105–106
  today, 149

P

Pack saddles, 80–82, 92*–93*
People of the King, 136–138
People of the Veil, 14
Phoenicians, 34
Population, 16

R

Raids, 38, 93–96, 105–106, 139
  code of, 95
  peace councils, 95
Rainfall, 21, 22, 25–26, 87
Religion, 38, 45, 117–131, 147–148
  Allah, 26, 117, 119, 121, 124
  animal sacrifices, 127, 131
  belief in afterlife, 124–125
  belief in supernatural, 125–126
  calendar, Moslem, 120
  early, 45
  holy men, 121–124
  instruction in, 67

Religion (cont.)
  Islam, 117, 119–121
  Koran, 117, 120, 122–124, 126
  Mohammed, 117, 119–120
  Moslem, 117–121, 147
  mosque, 117–118, 119, 147–148
  prayers, 117–119, 147
Rock paintings, 23, 28, 29–30, 31*, 36
  Tassili frescoes, 23, 29, 31*, 36
Rodd, Sir Francis Rennell, 147–149
Romans, 34, 35

S

Saddle, 57, 59*, 73–74
Sahara Desert, 17*, 150*
  description of, 20–36, 55
  early history, 28–36, 31*, 98–99
  farming in, 30–33, 98
  geology of, 99–100
  irrigation of, 98–101, 104–105
  mineral wealth, 149, 150*
  oases, 34, 97–99, 104–110, 149
  rainfall, 21, 22, 25–26, 87
  sandstorms, 22
Salt, 89–93, 135

SONIA BLEEKER (Mrs. Herbert S. Zim) was educated in the New York public schools and received her B.A. degree from Hunter College. She did graduate work in anthropology at Columbia University, under Franz Boas and Ruth Benedict.

In 1949, while looking for some books about Indians to read to her two sons, Miss Bleeker found there were very few at their age level and decided to write one herself. The result is her series of books on the American Indians, which began with *Indians of the Longhouse*, The Story of the Iroquois, published in 1950. Since then she has devoted her full time to writing and doing research for this series.

As a student, and later with her husband, Miss Bleeker crisscrossed the United States many times, concentrating on Indian country. She visited the Southeast, the entire length of the Pacific Coast and Canada, and the Southwest, and went across the border into Middle America. She has also traveled widely in Europe, and in 1961 made a trip around the world.

In the past several years Miss Bleeker has made three trips to Africa and has been doing extensive research for a series of books about Africa and its peoples for young readers. The first book, *The Masai, Herders of East Africa*, was published in 1963. *The Tuareg, Nomads and Warriors of the Sahara*, is the second book in the series.

Miss Bleeker and her family live on Plantation Key, Florida. Their home overlooks a vast, isolated stretch of the Atlantic Ocean. Some four miles out, between the Florida Reef and the north-flowing Gulf Stream, there is a busy lane for southbound ships. From her glass-walled study, Miss Bleeker can see their smoke-stacks and hulls against the horizon by day, and their glittering lights at night.